To Margaret Bill –
Love,
Dot   9/21/75

Helping Each Other In Widowhood

edited by

Phyllis R. Silverman
Dorothy MacKenzie
Mary Pettipas
Elizabeth Wilson

Harvard Medical School
Department of Psychiatry
Laboratory of Community Psychiatry

HEALTH SCIENCES PUBLISHING CORP.
New York, New York

Library of Congress Cataloging in Publication Data
Main entry under title:

Silverman, Phyllis R.
Helping each other in widowhood.
  1. Widows — United States. 2. Widowers — United States. 3.
Bereavement. 4. Consolation. I. Silverman, Phyllis R., ed.
HQ1058.5.U5H44   362.8′2   74-1284
ISBN 0-88238-519-4

Library of Congress Number — 74-1284

Printed in the United States of America by
MEILEN PRESS INC., NEW YORK, N. Y.

TABLE OF CONTENTS

PAGE

How It Is With Me Now (Poem) vii
    Alice Davis

Preface ix

Introduction xiii
    Elizabeth Wilson

Foreword xvii
    Gerald Caplan, M.D.

PART I: The Widow-to-Widow Program

Introduction 1

Chapter I—

    Background to the Development of the Widow-
    to-Widow Program 3
        Phyllis Silverman, Ph.D.

Chapter II—

    The Widow-to-Widow Program 17
        Dorothy MacKenzie

    Examples of Widow-to-Widow Visits I 24
        Adele Cooperband

    Examples of Widow-to-Widow Visits II 27
        Carrie Wynn

PAGE

Chapter III—

Who the Widow-to-Widow Program Served 31
Cécile Strugnell

Chapter IV—

The Widowed Service Line 51
Elizabeth Wilson

A Volunteer's Viewpoint 54
Arthur Churchill

Chapter V—

Who the Widowed Service Line Served 57
Ruby Abrams

Part II: How to Help Each Other

Introduction 73

Chapter VI—

Issues to Consider in Setting Up Outreach
Programs 75
Phyllis Silverman, Ph.D.

Chapter VII—

Organizations for the Widowed—Reports from
the Participants 83

Women's Fellowship Group, Church of the
Ascension, Rochester, New York 86
Mary Butterfield and Edith Kleisley

Catholic Widow and Widower Club, Hamilton,
Ohio 88
Mary Bell

Table of Contents

PAGE

Widows and Widowers Associated, Bridge-
port, Connecticut 90
    Catherine Stzurma

They Help Each Other Spiritually (THEOS),
Pittsburgh, Pennsylvania 94
    Bea Decker

Post Cana, Washington, D.C. 96
    Louise Duffy

Parents Without Partners, East Longmeadow,
Massachusetts 98
    Patricia H. Devine

Naim Conference, Chicago, Illinois 101
    Orville Plummer

Eschaton Club, Boston, Massachusetts 104
    Arthur Churchill

Carmel Club, Peabody, Massachusetts 105
    John Conlon

Chapter VIII—

Notes from the Conference for Widowed Only 107
    Ruby Abrahams and Cécile Strugnell

Chapter IX—

The Role of the Professional in a Mutual Help
Organization: Some Informal Ideas on This
Subject 127
Phyllis Silverman

Chapter X—

Preparing Volunteers 135

PART III: Death, Grief, and Bereavement:
The Professional Perspective

Introduction 143

Chapter XI—

Some Sociological Observations 147
Robert Fulton, Ph.D.

Chapter XII—

Some Observations by a Physician: Caring for
the Dying Patient and His Family 159
Melvin J. Krant, M.D.

Chapter XIII—

Some Observations by a Clergyman 171
Earl Grollman, D.D.

Chapter XIV—

The Role of the Funeral Director 187
Sumner James Waring, Jr.

EPILOGUE

Phyllis Silverman 203

Bibliography 207

HOW IT IS WITH ME NOW

By Alice J. Davis

From my beginning
I changed one hood
for another, design
and pattern shifting slowly
so that sometimes
I was unaware my hood
had slipped into different
style and texture—
batiste, soft wool, crisp cotton,
linen, and silk.

It is true I had to learn
to rearrange a fold or two
and some hoods were more
cumbersome than others.
When I learned to wear it,
I glorified in my wifehood,
cloth of gold with changing flecks
of color, sheer as a sari.

Ripping off my precious hood
the Hatter gone mad surely
clamped on a helmet
iron black and heavy
so heavy
I could not hold my head up. Tight
so tight
I could not breathe or hear or speak.

I was a long time
learning to wear
the most alien of all my hoods.
It sits lighter
on my shoulders now,
fabric softened and thinned
by tears and time,
blackness bleached
by sun and love of friends.

I thought
you would like to know
how it is with me now
after four years of wearing
this hood, which though easier
to bear, still
I hate.

PREFACE

The meetings reported in these pages were made possible by a special grant from the National Institute of Mental Health No. MH 09214 to the Laboratory of Community Psychiatry, Harvard Medical School. The Laboratory, under the direction of Gerald Caplan, M.D., is a teaching and research center concerned with developing preventive programs in mental health. Caplan pioneered in directing early efforts to help people forestall emotional problems. The Widow-to-Widow program is such a preventive effort and is one of the programs at the LOCP.

Psychiatrists and others in related work are not expert in helping people cope with normal life processes. Their experience is usually with the pathological. The future of preventive work to develop and maintain emotional well-being, may be with mutual groups such as the Widow-to-Widow program, groups which develop as individuals attempt to cope with these normal life crises, and use their experience to help others. Two workshops were held in the spring of 1971. The first was for Widows and Widowers only and the second was for Clergymen, Funeral Directors, and Mental Health Specialists who work with the bereaved. The purpose of these workshops was to develop the understanding and skills the participants needed to initiate new programs in their home communities.

One hundred widows and widowers from nineteen states took part in the first workshop. The participants included representatives from nine different groups for widowed people from various parts of the United States. The purpose of the workshop was to provide an opportunity for these various groups to share their experiences with each other, and to help those present to expand and/or develop new programs for the widowed in their communities. The focus was on the need to reach out to the newly widowed, following the model developed by the Widow-to-Widow experiment. The workshop brought together men and women who have coped with their own widowhood and the major change it brought to their lives. As their efforts are turned to helping others like themselves, some of whom may not be doing as well, they will contribute to the prevention of emotional disturbance.

The second workshop was for the purpose of educating professional workers about the needs of the widowed. Since these professionals were not widowed themselves, they lacked the same awareness of the problems created by the death of a spouse for the family involved. They are often called upon to help families at such times. By sensitizing them to these problems and alerting them to alternative modes of helping that might be available, we hoped to make them more effective during times of great upheaval for the families they serve. Professionals participated from family agencies, mental health clinics, and schools of theology. Several of the ministers were advisors to widowed groups. Two funeral directors from state organizations attended as well. The group had sufficiently various backgrounds to bring different points of view and perspectives to the discussions. Again, the focus was on the development of Widow-to-Widow programs in their home communities and on encouraging the use of the mutual help volunteer organizations as the means of providing service.

This book combines the proceedings of both workshops. The material has a broader appeal than to the limited audiences that were reached at these workshops and therefore we are presenting it in this formal manner in order to reach all who are concerned with the needs of the bereaved, and who want not only to understand the problem but to do something to help. We particularly hope that the material will be useful to widowed people who want to set up programs themselves and to others who may become widowed in the future. We hope, too, that this book will point the direction toward collaboration between mutual help groups and the professional health and welfare community.

A word of special thanks to Dr. Robert Fulton, Director of the Center for Death Education and Research, University of Minnesota, Dr. Melvin Krant, Director of Tufts University Medical Center Unit, Rabbi Earl Grollman, Spiritual Leader, Temple Beth-El Center, Belmont, Massachusetts, and Sumner Waring, President, Massachusetts Funeral Directors Association, for allowing us to include their talks in this volume. We are thus able to give the reader some perspective on the kinds of problems created by death for people in our society, and perspectives on how the physician, the clergy, and the funeral director respectively view these problems, and what they try to do about them.

Mrs. Alice Davis, whose poem begins this book, is a social worker and poet from Haverhill, Mass., who attended the second workshop. She has been widowed for 4 years. We are very grateful to her for allowing us to publish her poem in this volume.

A very special word of thanks to Mrs. Mary Pettipas who worked for three years as a widow's aide and then turned her attention to setting up these workshops. That they were well attended and successful is testimony to her organizational ability and her dedication to the ideas we tried to communicate.

The editors of this book have worked together since the inception of the Widow-to-Widow program. Phyllis Silverman, Ph.D., in Research and Social Welfare, did the background work that led to the development of the Widow-to-Widow program and served as its director. Dorothy MacKenzie, Mary Pettipas, and Elizabeth Wilson joined her to work as widow aides in the Widow-to-Widow program and then became program coordinators, taking on responsibility for the widowed service line that developed from the original program. We have come to know each other as friends and to work together as collaborators.

INTRODUCTION

By Elizabeth Wilson

Why The Need For Workshops About Widowhood

The idea of having a workshop probably started when a woman in Florida wrote to say she had read an article about our reach-out program to widows very recently bereaved. She had liked the idea, and had wanted to find out how to start such a program in her community. There followed others who also wanted to know if there were such programs in their area or if one could be started. They were concerned with what they needed to know as a widow in order to reach out to others who might need additional assistance.

We were acquainted with some of the existing groups around the country from studies made by Dr. Silverman before starting our program in Boston. We think that these various models for starting and maintaining widowed groups of mutual benefit should be shared, as different things are possible in different areas.

I would like to tell you some of my reasons for choosing to be involved in this program. When I became widowed, I was faced with the usual questions of self-identity, difficulties in seeing myself as a whole person, and in not being part of a team, but being a single parent. What did I want from life? What did society think of me now that I was widowed? How could I be comfortable in this coupled society in which we live?

The answers were slowly and painfully learned. In the process, I was helped most by other widowed people. The alternate ways of solving problems they suggested may not have been the ones I chose, but it was helpful to know that there was more than one method of resolution. The realization that, regardless of economic strata or ethnic background, the answers to these questions were difficult for all widowed people made me want to help others in these particular areas.

There were other things which irritated me—like the negativeness of the term "widowed." I tried other words. How about "unwidowed," "unmarried"? Many people just cannot understand what it means to be widowed. I feel that we who are widowed can do much to change this lack of understanding by our manner and by our willingness to let others know what we feel and what we would find helpful from them. Many times the isolation one feels is self-inflicted. There are some who might help, if given permission and direction. I see it as a very rewarding responsibility for us, who have managed to cope with and establish a different pattern of living, to help those who have not. One must know what is really needed, and how to go about getting it before one can move in a constructive way. Waiting for someone else to do it is never a good response. We know what our needs are and, by doing for ourselves and each other, these needs can be met.

It seems to me that would-be helpers to widowed people, whether professional or not, can do more by helping the widowed person do what he has to do himself, rather than by doing it for him. When one becomes widowed, the drive, purpose, and some of the ability seem to leave. It is most difficult to do even some simple things. In some ways he or she can be thought of as "going on" and may not at all be sure that he or she wants to do that. Widowed people find themselves so immersed in the misery of their situation that it seems as if nothing will ever be right again. Since everything seems out of whack for the new widow, help with decision-making by presenting alternatives can lend some perspective to the situation.

Needless to say we have been very excited by these gatherings. They have borne fruit beyond our fondest hopes. Our business was to develop ways of helping ourselves as widowed people and helping others who unfortunately join our ranks every day. This book provides the opportunity for both the widowed and non-widowed to understand something of the needs and problems of the widowed and gives some direction in setting up programs to meet these needs.

FOREWORD

By Gerald Caplan, M.D.

The death of a spouse is for most people a traumatic event that produces drastic changes in almost every aspect of life. In addition to the immediate pain, it leads to prolonged psychological and social burdens. Our Harvard researches have shown that this crisis and its aftermath increase the risk of mental and physical disorder in the survivors; these findings have been amply corroborated by others. We have also discovered that, as in other crises, the painful process of adjustment also provides an opportunity for many widows and widowers to gain in maturity, to develop psychologically, to be tempered by the fire.

Widowhood therefore presents a challenge to those of us who are concerned about reducing the rate of mental disorder and improving the level of psychological functioning in the community. Can we provide a support system for the widowed that will be widely acceptable as well as effective in helping them master the crises and complications of their fate, so that they may avoid its pitfalls and improve their mental competence?

Our approach to this question is based upon the conviction, as noted by Phyllis Silverman in her early exploratory work prior to developing a program, that the best units of such a support system are other widows and widowers. They have themselves successfully struggled with the trials and tribulations of the adjustment process and thus are more acceptable to the widowed and far more available than mental health specialists or other professional counsellors. This belief led us to establish our Widow-to-Widow program, which, in turn, resulted in the development of our

xvii

Widowed Service Line and other self-help activities. We utilized our talented professionals to support and guide, but not to direct these programs in any traditional sense.

We have been pleased with the results. Not only have our efforts benefited many newly widowed people, but those widows and widowers who contributed their time and energy to help others were themselves enriched psychologically and spiritually in the process. And we scientists learned a lot by observing and analyzing how non-professionals may help their fellows, often in ways that are different and more effective than the traditional methods of specialists. We have also learned, if we accept seriously our community mental health mission to cater to the entire population, that the way to deal with the large numbers of people involved, is to keep spinning off new self-help groups, so that those who have been helped may in turn help others. This has led us logically to the plan to stimulate an extension of this approach on a widespread scale throughout the country, a plan that is made more feasible by the fact that during the last few years several groups in other places have had experiences similar to our own and have also become eager to foster a country-wide movement.

The conferences that we organized were the next steps. This book attempts to communicate what took place there to a wider audience than those who attended. It is no ordinary conference report, but a message of challenge and hope to all widows and widowers. I hope that many will read it and that it will arouse in some of them the wish to develop similar projects in their own localities.

PART I

The Widow-to-Widow Program

Introduction

Part I is devoted to the presentation of the work of the Widow-to-Widow program so that the reader can gain from its experience and not repeat its mistakes. It begins with a history of the Widow-to-Widow program written by Phyllis Silverman, describing the idea of an outreach program and how it was developed to become a mutual help effort in which the widowed helped each other. Dorothy MacKenzie, Adele Cooperband and Carrie Wynn, all of whom are widowed and worked as aides in the original Widow-to-Widow experiment, prepared the next chapter.

Mrs. MacKenzie describes what it was like to reach out to new widows, to see them in their own homes, and to offer friendship, moral support and guidance from her own experience as a widow. Mrs. Wynn and Mrs. Cooperband provide some concrete examples of the situations they encountered in the two and one-half years they worked on the program. These personal stories are composites prepared for the workshops so as to protect the privacy of the women helped by the program. Cecile Strugnell, a sociologist, who worked as a research assistant with the Widow-to-Widow program, reports in succinct fashion some of what was learned from this work, who was served, who refused, and so forth. This kind of perspective can come from an experimental program as was ours, but has value only if it is used to improve the program, to reach more people in a way which is more helpful to them.

In addition to the outreach program, there is a report on the telephone "hot line" manned by volunteer widows and widowers which the widowed called to ask for help. The line was administered by Elizabeth Wilson and Dorothy MacKenzie. Mrs. Wilson describes its inception. Arthur Churchill, a volunteer, talks about his experience. Ruby Abrahams, a sociologist, who worked as a research associate with the service line, reports on what was learned from this program.

Chapter I

BACKGROUND TO THE DEVELOPMENT OF THE WIDOW-TO-WIDOW PROGRAM

By Phyllis Silverman, Ph.D.

A history of the Widow-to-Widow program is not complete without a few sentences on how I, as a non-widowed person, came to be involved in this work. It began as a job which I reluctantly accepted. Dr. Gerald Caplan was interested in knowing more about the available services in the formal health and welfare system for the newly widowed individual, and what services might be provided which would best meet the needs of the widowed. I had long been interested in how the consumer of services evaluated the help he received and which help he considered most useful, but I felt ill-suited to work with bereaved people. When I went by a cemetery, I closed my eyes and I could not talk about death. Dr. Caplan encouraged me to look into what services were available, and only because of my interest in the broader issue did I agree. I never regretted that decision.

Let me define health and welfare, or as they are being called today, the human services network. This is where I started my study. Included in human services are psychiatric clinics, OPD, and in part, community mental health centers, child guidance clinics, school guidance programs, hospital social service departments, welfare departments, health centers, and so forth. Lawyers and physicians in private practice might be included here, as well as community centers, settlements and the like. At the end I included clergy and funeral directors; normally we do not categorize them as members of the health and welfare network. However, when dealing with death, the funeral directors are the only people who know what to do when burying the dead and can be very crucial to helping the family get through this trying time. Clergymen, too, are present at every funeral. In short, my mandate was to find to whom widows and widowers turn for what kind of help and what they expected would be offered and I sought out any conceivable caregiver that might be involved.

I learned that, for the most part, these caregivers were inadequate. Not only did they have little understanding of what a widow or widower needs, but more often than not, they would withdraw, advising the bereaved to keep a "stiff upper lip." Family and friends were relieved when they left the bereaved to manage on his own. The physician offered a tranquilizer to calm the nerves, but no real understanding. The clergyman had platitudes; he was of little comfort.

I tried to combine the findings on services with what I knew about mourning. As a result of the work of such people as John Bowlby (1961) of England and James Tyhurst (1958) of Canada, it was possible to describe grief as a process, a series of stages through which the individual went. Each successive stage required a different service. I then matched services with the needs of each stage. The stages of mourning can be divided into three phases: impact, recoil and accommodation.

The Initial Phase:

During the initial impact phase, the individual mourner is described as experiencing a sense of being lost and of not knowing what to do next. They feel suspended from life, are unable to concentrate, and are indifferent to their immediate needs. That the deceased is truly gone holds no reality for them.

The initial caregiver, and a participant in *every* bereavement, is the funeral director. He knows about burying the deceased; he often initiates the Social Security application; and he can be relatively helpful in many ways depending on his personal inclination and who else is available to help at the time of the funeral.

Family and friends play a most active role at this time. They may stay in the household, take over the housekeeping temporarily, be available to provide moral and emotional support, and give the bereaved a feeling of not being completely alone.

Clergymen are the other universal caregivers during the bereavement period. It is common practice that a clergyman officiates at a funeral. If the family has no preference, then the funeral director invites a member of the clergy. When asked, all clergymen felt that they should do more, not only about modifying funeral practices, but about being involved with the mourners. For their failure to do so, they offered the following excuses: lack of time, failure of the bereaved to make direct demands for help to remind them of their need, uncertainty as to the type of support that would be most beneficial.

The clergy felt that the time immediately after a death— other than for homemaking service or financial aid—was not the critical period of need; many family members and friends were still available. Usually, however, within a month after the death, relatives, friends and neighbors have moved back to their own lives. It is then that the bereaved person, left by himself to deal with his new life

5

situation, may specifically need someone with whom to talk over his problems and plans.

Lawyers generally have a limited formal role to play in the recovery from bereavement for any given family. Their role is most important where there is an estate to settle, which generally occurs in the more affluent families.

Other than insurance or inherited money in addition to her own earning capacity, there are two sources of financial support available for the widow, Social Security and Public Welfare. Public Welfare is based on a means test. To be eligible, the widow must have established residency and have limited financial resources within the maximum prescribed by law.

If a family is receiving Social Security and the total income falls below a certain level established by law, they are eligible for supplemental benefits from public assistance. There are several categories of aid established under federal law. In cases of need, whether the family is known to them or not, welfare will provide funds (up to $400) to cover burial costs. The widow does not receive any special service other than what is available to other welfare recipients. She is not differentiated by the agency from the woman who is divorced or separated. Agencies such as settlement houses offer baby-sitting service to members, and other programs for children; family agencies can provide *temporary* homemaking service (although this is an area of permanent need which perhaps only the widowed can arrange for themselves). The Visiting Nurse Association, when they were involved with bed-side care of the deceased, sometimes remain to help a family make plans. The list of lodges, fraternal organizations, and unions, is endless and the friendship and financial assistance they may provide is invaluable.

Development of the Widow-to-Widow Program

The U.A.W., in Detroit, studied the adequacy of their benefits to the widows of their members. A similar study has been completed by the insurance industry. Invariably widowhood involved a lowering of the families' standard of living.

There are services available from family, clergy, and agencies to meet many of the needs of widowed people during the impact period. However, people do not always know of, nor avail themselves of, these services. Often because of his emotional state, the newly widowed person is limited in his capacity to determine his own need and take the initiative to find the right service.

The Recoil Phase:

This second phase, not always distinct in its differentiation from the impact phase, can cover a period of time extending from one month, one year, or even longer after the death.

The widowed report experiencing their loss most acutely during this period, because the numbness has left and the ability to feel returns. Some report a period of trying to function exactly as the deceased would have liked, as if trying to recapture him in spirit, if not in fact. This may be normal at the funeral; it is the deceased whose wishes and presence dominate the occasion.

A need to talk about the deceased and to review the facts of his death can become an obsession, to the annoyance of friends and relatives. Anger and sometimes frightening, irrational feelings about the tricks life has played can come out with greater intensity, often more frightening to the audience than to the widowed person himself. During this time, the widowed person experiences acute periods of loneliness; and even when in company knows no relief. The widowed also report that they begin to move away from their married friends; they resent the sympathy and they begin to feel like a fifth wheel. They see themselves as different (defective) from their previous social network, since they are no longer part of a couple.

During the early part of this period, relationships with family and friends return to normal. The bereaved person usually begins to emerge from the fog, takes charge of himself and his family again, and, at least superficially, appears to be "carrying on."

The concrete tasks that are required are those of planning for and maintaining the household. Some women may consider finding a job and becoming the breadwinner as important as being the home-maker. A man with dependent children may need a home-maker, or he may move in with relatives.

One is tempted to speculate that it may be easiest for the widowed person to become fixated at this stage in the bereavement process. While the individual may make an adjustment that permits him to carry on, his activities may be more related to his past and to the deceased than to a future in which he has given up the deceased as a central person in his life. As one widow said to me:

> It took me a long time before I realized that I was cleaning to please my husband and it didn't matter to him anymore. That really made me stop and think. It was a turning point for me.

Members of clubs for widowed people report that without some additional assistance they would not have been able to move beyond the second phase of mourning, which lasted at least a year.

There seem to be very few people available wtih whom the widowed individual can talk during this period. Many people report preferring to talk to other widowed people, who seem more willing to listen than most. It is not easy to find a helpful audience.

David Maddison, (1968) an Australian psychiatrist, did a survey of whom new widows found most helpful during the first year after their husbands died. This study confirmed that most widows felt other widows most helpful. Professional mental health workers report experiencing great discomfort when clients exhibit the depth of their despair and grief. They attribute this to the acute awareness they develop of their own vulnerability to becoming widowed. The anxiety about experiencing the intense feelings a bereaved person displays may be why clergymen back away, why families advocate a "stiff upper lip," and why another widowed person is reported to be the most helpful caregiver during this period.

The clergy report that this is the period during which they know least what to do. Their parishioners may appear to be having serious emotional difficulty that could require specialized service.

One way to respond to the bereaved's stressful behavior is to call it an emotional illness and refer him to a psychiatric agency or clinic. I did not find that making such referrals of newly bereaved people to be a general practice if you study the caseloads of psychiatric clinics. This may in part be due to the stigma attached to seeking casework or psychiatric help; it may also be a result of the widowed being more accepting of grief as a natural part of the bereavement and not a sign of disorder; or, they may not be aware that such services exist.

It would seem then, that during this recoil phase, there are very few special services available for the widowed that would give them an opportunity to talk, to mourn, and to find their way into the future.

The Period of Accommodation:

The recovery period is a time of looking to the future. This can occur any time within three months to two years after the death. The emotional tasks involve letting go of the past, giving up a relationship to a spouse and building a new life as a single person. This means learning to be alone and finding a meaningful, social and emotional life in addition to being head of a household with all its attendant responsibilities. This is the hardest period to describe; whatever adjustment an individual will make depends on his life style, education and personality. In fact, mental health professionals know least about this period. The people seen are often those who have not recovered. Many of the members of the widows' groups seem to be examples of people who have made new adjustments.

In my travels, I discovered several widowed groups: Naim, Post Cana, Theos. I was fortunate enough to visit Post Cana and this, plus the data from Maddison's work, made it very clear to me that another widow has a unique contribution to make. She provides patience, perspective and understanding. These groups offered the most effective and singular service in helping the widowed recover.

Developing the Program:

The primary interest of the Laboratory of Community Psychiatry is in developing programs to prevent mental illness. I do not like the word "illness" but instead would use the word "distress." Let me offer a definition of emotional distress. It is an inability to cope with a life situation in which an individual finds himself. A child afraid to go to school and leave his mother has an emotional problem. A child who never successfully becomes independent of his parents may develop chronic disabilities which may make it impossible to cope with life as an adult in his own right. Prevention would occur at first grade or kindergarten with some help to get him to school and to guide his parents in helping him grow. What kind of intervention, and how to get to the person in trouble, are questions we are still trying to answer.

A newly-widowed person is, at least temporarily, in a precarious emotional condition. More than we would expect (all together, still a very small number for their proportion in the general population) end up seeking psychiatric help.

What kind of program should be developed to avoid this end? Talking prevention is talking public health. It is had to know *who* to vaccinate when preventing smallpox; some people have a natural immunity. To be sure that no one will be missed, everyone gets vaccinated or immunized. Is it possible to call on everyone who is widowed? Some people may need extra help to get by while others may be fine over the long haul of changing, accommodating, making the necessary adjustments to the enormously tragic and terrible fact that their spouse has died.

If one comes as a social worker to offer help to the bereaved, one would be irrelevant. Perhaps a psychiatrist would only verify the fears an upset widow has that she is, indeed, going crazy. Another widow, or widower, a neighbor, would possibly be more welcome and have something tangible and more meaningful to offer. Using the theory that another widow or widower would be most helpful and regarding them as having a legitimacy to call on a newly bereaved person, we developed the idea of the Widow-to-Widow program. These people were not to be psychotherapists or junior social workers; they would be people who could offer friendship, understanding and guidance and, if they came to call, might indeed be accepted.

The idea was good—but the difficulty was how to begin. We chose a community where we would have a chance to serve enough widows to demonstrate the value of what we were doing. This was a community of 250,000 people, where about 200 women, under the age of 60, were widowed in a year. We wanted to serve people from different backgrounds and in sufficient numbers to see if the idea worked. However, we were not primarily a research project but a service organization. If there was any research, it would take second place and serve only to determine whether or not the service worked.

As a service group in a given community, Harvard provided no legitimation. People would perhaps think that we wanted to use them as guinea pigs. In addition, if the idea worked, Harvard could not provide a permanent service of this sort in any community. Thus, grass-root ties were needed in a setting which would allow a mutual help organization to develop. A community synagogue, a Y.M.C.A. which had connections in the black community and the white Protestant communities, and a Catholic Archdiocesan group (the Council of Catholic Men and Women) were chosen. Unfortunately, we chose sponsors who were as poor as church mice, and, while they gave legitimation (up to a point), they could not give any permanent organizational support. They did help to recruit the women who became widow aides and they did make policy decisions about how we would proceed in their community.

Five women were employed. They could not participate on a voluntary basis because of the large size of the community and because this was a demonstration program which might involve more time. They were receiving social security and all were able to work part-time. My criteria for hiring them was that they had been widowed long enough to talk about it with some objectivity, that they had enough perspective to use their experience to help others, and that they were pleasant and attractive women who made it easy to know them. They all lived in or near the community to be served and could easily be identified as a friend or neighbor by the new widow. I did not consider this to be a time for ecumenism or integration; I preferred that they call on people from their own backgrounds. I therefore chose one Negro, one Jewish and three Catholic women—generally reflecting the proportion of people with these backgrounds in this community. These women had all worked in the recent past; one as a saleswoman, one as a legal secretary, and so forth. None of them had ever done this kind of helping before, although they had been involved as volunteers in community organizations and had helped widowed friends on an informal basis.

The remainder of this Section of the book describes the details of what we did once the aides were recruited. Let me briefly characterize the two programs we developed.

The Widow-to-Widow program reaches out to people at a time when they are at their weakest moment—often in crisis. Yet, not everyone needs or wants help. It was found that those with dependent children at home most regularly accepted the aide. Many women said that they were fine—but were, in fact, still in shock, and only later were pleased to see the aide when everything did fall apart. They had not expected this to happen, and it was of value that she had continued to call from time to time.

The Widowed Service Line, focused more on long-term, residual difficulties. This program began as the Widow-to-Widow program phased out. This line permitted us to reach a larger geographic area and to serve both men and women. It was staffed by volunteers who were widows and widowers.

How did the line come about? I'm not sure. Hot lines are very much in the news these days. With the dwindling of funds for the Widow-to-Widow demonstration, several of the aides thought that this approach, while still adhering to the concept of Widow-to-Widow, could extend to many more communities and include men and women. They had found the telephone a very useful tool for being available at all times in the Widow-to-Widow program. With many women, whom they could not visit for one reason or another, they developed close friendships and were very helpful on the telephone. Such a service would be relatively inexpensive compared to other aspects of the program and might easily be housed in a social agency. A grant from the National Institute of Mental Health relieved the financial strain for a year and the "line" was started.

The line reached fewer *newly* widowed people, however; they generally don't have the energy to reach out and ask for help. We are learning a good deal about the complex problems for which other people have found no solutions. The importance of early outreach and the need to be readily available to a bereaved individual soon after their spouse dies is being substantiated by this experience. We have also come to appreciate how different people's needs are at different points in the bereavement process.

DISCUSSION NOTES

The discussion began with a question about the degree of suspicion people had when they were first offered help. However, suspicion turned out not to be a major factor in people's response. Many people who said, "No," had not yet experienced a need for intervention from anyone outside of their family. This led to the question of how to make the program known to people who might need assistance. The value of using the funeral director was emphasized. It was pointed out that he knew every bereaved family; that we often do not think of him as a referral source, but people do trust him and would accept his advice if he told them about the service. Referrals, in fact, could come from many sources such as parish registries, obituary columns and the like. Another way of getting referrals was suggested; that is publicizing the program in local newspapers, and on radio and T.V. It was pointed out that this brings people to the organization, but in an outreach program where the group offers help to someone unsolicited, other means have to be found to locate the bereaved. The funeral director, or registry of vital statistics could be helpful here.

A final question was raised about why the Widow-to-Widow experiment reached only widows. The advisory groups of clergymen in the target community did not feel

15

that widows could reach out to widowers without their intentions being questioned. It was never possible to recruit a widower to work with us in this program. Both widows and widowers worked on the service line and calls were received from both men and women. Once a program is established in the community, such issues may not be so critical, but in trying something new it is very important not to do anything that could be misunderstood.

Chapter II

THE WIDOW-TO-WIDOW PROGRAM

By Dorothy MacKenzie

The Widow-to-Widow program became reality because it was apparent that it was not a professional social worker who could be most helpful to new widows but, rather, other widows who had made new lives for themselves. Dr. Silverman recruited the original five widows' aides from Parents Without Partners, existing widow groups and community-oriented organizations. The community chosen for the Widow-to-Widow program was Dorchester, Mass., a heterogeneous, predominantly Catholic, lower-middle class section of Boston. On the premise that the new widow would be more comfortable with an aide of her own religious background, three Catholics, one Negro and one Jew were hired as the widows' aides. The white Protestant widows were served by the Catholic aides. The main requirement for this job was to have successfully adjusted to our own widowhood and to be willing to help a new widow make this adjustment. We would draw on our own experiences as widows to help the newly widowed woman bridge the gap from a married woman to a widow.

After about five or six meetings with Dr. Silverman during which we explored how best to approach the new widows (we already had the death certificates from the Bureau of Vital Statistics in Boston), we decided to send a letter to the newly widowed about three weeks after her husband's death. Three weeks after the death seemed to be an appropriate time to reach out; usually, by then, the family and close friends of the new widow had returned to their own business and felt she should do the same, implying if not stating, it was time for her to start making a new life. In the letter, we gave the date and time we would visit at her home. Had it been left up to the widow to make the appointment, she probably would not have done so. However, we did include our phone number in the event she would not be home or did not want, or feel any particular need, to have us visit her.

How we labored over that letter! We wanted it to be perfect. Needless to say, there were countless revisions, but we finally came up with a version we thought appropriate—short, sweet, and to the point, but getting across the message that we wanted to be helpful. This letter was written on informal note paper which said Widow-to-Widow Program on the top and listed the community sponsors on the side. We did not mention Harvard, thinking people would be put off by this, and assume that we wanted to do research on them. In retrospect, the widows we served said they were pleased to be associated with Harvard, and would not have thought about it as research. The letter, with some variations, went as follows:

Dear Mrs. ——————————————:

Having learned of your recent loss, I would like to visit you.

Since I too am a widow and know how comforting it is to talk to someone who is in the same situation, I would like to call on you on (date) at (time), if this is convenient for you. If not, please call me at (home phone number) and we can make other arrangements.

Sincerely,

It should be noted here that the initial reaction on the part of some of the widows to our letter was suspicion— "What is she trying to sell?"—"Where did she get my name?"—and so forth. Once they saw us in person or talked to us on the phone, we were able to quickly allay their fears that we had an ulterior motive. In those instances where we had been able to make use of a personal reference from someone known to them, such as a member of the clergy, or a funeral director, we were always accepted.

What follows are some examples of how we helped. We did not realize it but, in the situations we chose to share with you, we did not contact these widows by letter. This seems to prove that, for every rule, there is an exception. The aide was introduced by an interested third party and the letter became unnecessary. The letter seems most important when there is no other way of being introduced to the new widow.

On the strength of this observation, Betty Wilson contacted personally clergymen of all the churches and synagogues in the Dorchester area, to make them aware of our program, and to ask them to refer new widows of their parish or congregations to us. They never followed through.

The problem of introduction is one that needs further consideration. We have thought that funeral directors might be asked to include among the information they give widows at the time of the funeral, a notice about such a service as ours so that it would not be totally unknown to them when contacted by the aide. Although the funeral directors agreed with this in theory, it was never put into practice. This may not be a problem for those working in smaller communities where one is already an active participant.

I remember so well my first call. I had written to the new widow, explained who I was, my reason for wanting to see her, and told her the date and time of my visit. Since I had not heard from her, I assumed she wanted to see me. I set out on that first call with some misgivings: "What would it be like?" "Could I really help her?" "What would I say?" When I arrived at her home, no one was there. It was quite a blow! There I was, ready to save the world —and nobody wanted to be saved!

After about three or four similar experiences, I finally had my first face-to-face meeting with a new widow. This widow had no particular problems, but I was so pleased that, at last, I had made a home visit in the Widow-to-Widow program.

Although we did not actually see all of these widows after making that first contact, we were able to be very helpful to many of them through lengthy phone conversations. More often than not, if the widow was not going to be home for our visit, she would call and say so and suggest that perhaps we could get together another time. During the course of these phone conversations, as well as the home visits, the widow would tell us many things about the problems of trying to make a new life: financial difficulties, lack of understanding from members of her family, children suddenly getting poor grades in school, not being able to eat or sleep properly, feeling so lost and lonely and fearful of having to make so many decisions, where, before her husband's death, she never had to make any. One young widow with small children whom I did visit in her home, told me in a subsequent phone conversation that she had sold her three-family home and bought a new single-family house in a different community. Prior to this, the biggest decision she had had to make was, "Should I buy a loaf of bread today or not?"

During the months of these home visits and phone conversations, we acquired a great deal of expertise in knowing what questions to ask, how best to put the widow at ease, and how to express our real desire to help. For many of these widows, it was such a relief to be able to give voice to their feelings about their husband's death and their fears for the future, without being put off. They welcomed the opportunity to unburden themselves to an understanding person, someone who was not directly involved in their lives. Too often, well-meaning clergy, family and friends had told them to keep a stiff upper lip, that life must go on, and so forth—and this is not what a newly widowed person wants to hear. Along with the moral support, we were able to give them some much needed practical information, in addition to sharing our own experiences and feelings as widows.

Early in the program, we realized that many of the women who received our letter did not need us. They were getting all the support necessary from their families and close friends, which often included a widow. However, we did keep their names on our mailing list and periodically sent them notices of meetings that were planned which might interest them. As a result of these meetings, we did get to meet some of the widows who had initially turned down our offer of help—they didn't need us then, but six months or a year later, they were so glad we had kept in touch. Some very solid and still ongoing friendships among the widows themselves and between the aides and the widows are one of the happy results of the Widow-to-Widow Program.

During the entire three years of this effort, we met once a week with Phyllis Silverman and the research staff, to document our work. This part of the work interested us the least, as aides—research wasn't our "thing"—we were more concerned with helping. These weekly meetings, however, were extremely important. We needed the give-and-take of these sessions for our own moral support. We talked about our calls—some that were especially troublesome—had we handled them properly, was there more we could have done, were there other resources available to fill a particular need of the new widow? One of the beneficial aspects of these meetings to us, as non-professionals doing something we had never done before, was the knowledge that we had the full support and backing of the professionals at the Laboratory of Community Psychiatry.

When this phase of the Widow-to-Widow Program ended, it was very satisfying to know that our efforts did, indeed, contribute much to the well-being of many newly-widowed women and that there was one common denominator which helped make it work; we shared the bond of widowhood.

In the Dorchester pilot program, we visited widows only. We did not minimize the needs of widowers, but agreed that, for the moment, it was more important to demonstrate that such a program could work.

We did try to enlist the services of a widower who would reach out. The men who were interested worked full time and could do this only in the evening. It would have been impossible to provide them with the back-up they would need. Our program was geared to suit the needs of the aides as working mothers and, at the time, none of us wanted to be involved in any extra evening work. With the development of the Service Line, we did set up a format which could accommodate to the needs of volunteers who have full-time jobs.

Examples of Widow-to-Widow Visits I

By Adele Cooperband

I was asked to help a bereaved widow who was under psychiatric treatment. I couldn't imagine what I could do when a professional person couldn't help. I have since visited her many times and have spent long hours on the telephone with her, and she has changed a great deal. She is fine today, and has a warm relationship with her children.

After the funeral, the widow had moved into her sister's house and the sister had sent her own daughter to sleep in the widow's house with her children; two households were disrupted.

The children were understandably upset. The son seemed to be calm and tolerant of his mother; the daughter was emotional and intolerant. She had been very close to her father and felt his loss greatly, and the lack of her mother's understanding created a dreadful situation.

Let me describe my first visit. We sat in her sister's playroom; and Mrs. Smith talked, cried, and I listened. She repeated many times how good, kind and generous her husband had been and there was no other like him, and never would be. At that point, I intervened and told her not to canonize her husband in front of the children because she would make them feel they had not just lost their father, but that they had lost an angel. The sister made a remark that she could not stand his ways, and said: "You two argued plenty." Then Mrs. Smith told me that her husband would work long hours and this did displease her. I said: "Don't berate yourself for that. It is very natural to be displeased and argue sometimes."

24

By that time it was 1:00 p.m., and I was getting hungry and said that I was going to leave. She asked me to stay and said she would make a sandwich for me. I declined and, instead, asked her to accompany me to a restaurant so that both of us could have lunch. In this way she got out of the house for a while as well. On our way back, I asked her to show me where she lived, and when we got near the house I asked her to show me the inside. While we were inside, I asked her if she had some work that she would like to do while we were talking. She said she could put in a wash as she had not done any laundry since she had been in her sister's home. We went down to the basement and she put in the wash.

We stayed in her house until about 5:00 p.m., then I brought her back to her sister's. She asked me to come again and I told her that if she would go back to her own home, then I would visit her often. We talked several times on the phone and she did go back home to live.

Her children liked and respected me. Every time I left the house and went into my car, the daughter followed me and sat and talked to me: "If only Mom would smile or say something kind; I haven't heard laughter since Daddy died." I told the children to be patient with their mother. When their father was alive, the two of them shared the responsibility; now she had no one to share it with and it is very hard to manage alone. I urged them to try to be understanding, explaining that she would change eventually. To Mrs. Smith I would say: "Try to laugh once in a while at the children's jokes, say something kind to them. Children who don't hear laughter or a kind word grow up with warped characters"—something she wouldn't want to see. Her children were really "good kids."

Many months later I encouraged Mrs. Smith to start driving a car and to seek part-time employment. Today, she is dating, working, and is more understanding of her children and able to say how proud she is of them. The children, who were doing poorly at school, are now doing well again. She still calls me on the average of once a week to talk with me about what is going on in the family.

Examples of Widow-to-Widow Visits II

By Carrie Wynn

One of the first widows I visited had been referred to me by the local minister. She was about forty-five years old and had a twelve-year old son. The minister told me she was having a hard time, and would I go and see her? So I dropped in on her.

I told her I belonged to the Widow-to-Widow Program and I knew her minister and he had told me about her. She asked me if I were a widow and how many children I had and, pretty soon, we were sitting at the kitchen table with a cup of coffee.

She told me that her husband had been very sick with cancer for the last three years. For the last year, when he was so sick, she had to do everything to look after him. When I asked her how things were for her, she said: "I will be honest with you, it's been pretty rough. We were very, very close. He did everything for us, he did not want me to work." Then she went on to tell me how he had been in the bedroom sick for such a long time, even though he did not die there. She could not bring herself to go into the bedroom since he died (this was about three weeks earlier). So I told her:

> I know what you mean about not wanting to go into the bedroom. I did not want to go into the bedroom either. But one night I had to get some papers that were there, so I went in, and I just felt so funny I sat down and cried and cried. The kids heard me; they came in and said: 'Why are you sitting there crying? You said you weren't going to go into the bedroom.'

I had not meant to stay there, but all of a sudden I went to pieces.

After telling her how I had felt, I added:

You will see, something will take you back in there, too. It will just come on you all of a sudden and the next thing you know you will be walking right in there.

A few days later I called her up and asked her how she was doing. She said to me: "You know something? After you left, I don't know what you said to me, but in the next couple of days after you were here, I went into the room." I said: "That is wonderful." She also told me how she had spoken to her sister about me: "I told her I have never talked to anyone like you before. I don't know what you said to me, but it just brought something out of me."

She told me about a job she was thinking of taking, and I told her it would be good for her, to take her out of the home. She is now very busy teaching and active in community work. I still drop in on her when I am in the neighborhood. She is always glad to see me.

Another widow I have been in touch with was a person I had been neighbors with many years ago. I knew her husband, too, and had some idea of the kind of problems they had.

When I called her, she was very glad to hear from me, and we both talked about our husbands. She opened up quite a bit about how she had felt about him, and yet, how she was missing him now that he was gone.

This widow was working, but, after a while, she lost her job, and she took to visiting me fairly regularly on her way to the unemployment office. Most of her problems were with the youngest of her four children—a fifteen-year-old boy. The others were married or had regular jobs. This boy had been a problem before her husband died, but now he was worse. He got into trouble with other kids for stealing cars. He was gone from home for a whole month, and she did not know where he was. She discovered that he had taken a job, not telling them about his age. She had to go to the probation officer to explain things to him. She had to go to the school asking them to take him back. One reason for his behavior was that he felt bad about not having been a better son and closer to his father while he was alive.

This boy had gotten into a bad crowd and begged his mother to move out of the neighborhood, so he could get away from it all and have another chance. I told her, "He is asking you to help him break away from his crowd. Why don't you look for somewhere else to live?" I helped her put her name on the waiting lists for two different projects. The area where she lived was really rough.

She came to see me quite a few times, so I guess she found it helpful to talk to me, especially as she know I understood how she was feeling about her husband, and it was good for her to talk these things out. (I have not yet heard whether she has managed to move, but I will be in touch, and I know her boy is in school).

Chapter III

WHO THE WIDOW-TO-WIDOW
PROGRAM SERVED

By Cecile Strugnell

What you have read so far will have given you some knowledge of how the program worked and a feeling for its spirit. Here, I will present some facts about who accepted us, what their needs were, how we tried to help them, and finally who refused us and for what reasons.

Our information was taken from the death certificates, the reports of the aides in the course of their service, and two sets of interviews conducted later, one with widows who refused us and the other with widows we had helped over a period of time.

Over a period of approximately two and one-half years in which the program operated, we tried to reach a total of 430 widows. This was the total number of women whose husbands were under 65 who became widowed in this period.

In organizing our information for a statistical analysis, we selected those widows who had first been approached by the service at least a year before. This limited us to the first 300 cases. Those people visited more recently, however, provided additional illustrative data.

We interviewed as many of these women who did not want to see us as we could, to learn their reasons for refusing, how they had handled their problems, and whether they had, at some later date, wished for help such as the aide might have provided.

In order to get a clearer picture of how the aide helped where she was accepted, we interviewed, in depth, 35 (25%)

of the widows who had had fairly extensive contacts with the service.

Who accepted, who refused:

Of the 300 widows we tried to reach, 67 were not available either because they had moved, the address did not exist, or no one had ever heard of them (In Dorchester, people are often fearful and will not pass on any information about their neighbors.) Several widows had been separated from their husbands for a long time before their deaths. In the black community, we failed to reach a number of widows because the aide who should have seen them was sick for a time, and because rioting made it unsafe to visit during the summer of 1968. These various reasons reduced the number of widows under study to 233. Of this number, 61% accepted our service to some extent.

Although Dorchester is mostly a working class community, 17.6% of our widows' husbands might be considered middle class, having either managerial or professional occupations (based on the occupational classification of the U.S. Census).

The job classification of the husbands of our widows was the following:

Professional, Managerial:	17.6%	(52.6% accepted)
Craftsmen, Salesmen:	28.2%	(60.7% accepted)
Clerical, Service Workers:	24.1%	(57.7% accepted)
Operatives, laborers and other	30.1%	(66.2% accepted)

Although statistically not significant, the difference in percentage of acceptance between the higher socio-economic group (52.6) and the lower (66.2) may mean that there was a greater range of opportunities and choices available to them which enables them to draw on other resources for help. It is important to keep in mind, however, that 52.6% did accept and that this is a large percentage indicating need.

Neither race nor religion seemed to have any influence on our being accepted or refused once we were able to reach a widow. Of the 233 we reached, 92.2% were white, and 8.8% were black. The white population was divided according to religious affiliation in the following manner: 59.2% Catholic, 10.3% Protestant, 17.5% Jewish, 13% religion unknown. The small percentage of blacks reached, (only 8.8%) is worthy of notice, as in contrast they represented 34% of the population we failed to contact. This high proportion reflects the environmental factors which made initial contact to offer our services much more difficult in the black community.

The death certificate gave us the age of the husband at death. As the widow's age was often difficult to ascertain, we decided to divide our population into age groups according to the husband's age, assuming that husband and wife would be approximately the same age.

Age of Husband at Death		*% Accepting Us.*
Under 40:	9.5%	81.8%
41-50	15.6%	61.1%
51-60	42.0%	62.9%
61-65	32.9%	51.3%

The younger widows were definitely more eager to receive our help than the older ones.

This finding becomes more meaningful if we look at a more significant factor; the presence of children. 81.3%

of the widows who had children under 16 years did accept us, as opposed to 58% of those without. The younger the woman was, the younger the children were, the more likely our help was to be welcome in the early stages of contact.

Though an older woman may not feel the extent of the crisis of widowhood right away, the young widow immediately finds herself in a situation which is quite unusual in her age group. She is confronted in a more brutal fashion with what widowhood will mean to her. She has no peers in the same situation. She does not know how to relate to the single friends she may still have, as they have never been married. Relationships with her married friends are difficult as she is now single. Isolated in her own emotional needs, she also is alone in facing the needs of her children. In our experience the family proves to be of limited help to the young widow, and often antagonizes her by lack of understanding. In contrast, our aide could find natural and easy openings when talking to a young widow for the first time. By talking of the children, and referring to her own experience with bringing up her family alone, she invites the widow to share her concerns and worries. The young widow in turn is eager to find out how the aide managed, what difficulties she encountered. She wants to gain some perspective on what could happen, what it would feel like. By identifying with the aide who has raised young children, she begins to experience the reality of her widowhood and understand her new role.

The presence of young children in a family often contributes to making this family open to outside neighborly relationships, and therefore more open to the relationship offered by the aide, which is similar to a friendly, neighborly approach. A widow with young children is also tied to the home and is eager for the opportunity to talk to another adult, to get out of the home and to meet other people. These are some of the needs the aide tries to fill (Silverman, 1971).

Another factor that seemed relevant to our being accepted or not was whether the wife was working at the time of bereavement. The aide was accepted by 76% of those not working, but only by 51% of those who worked. (A few women did change their work status as a result of bereavement; eight left their jobs to be able to stay home with the children. Twenty-two went to work, this decision often being made a while after their bereavement and frequently with the help and support of the aide). On the whole, it did seem that the non-working woman was more ready to accept us. One obvious reason is that being at home she was easier to reach and had more time to let the aide visit her. Another reason is that the housewife had often been totally dependent on her husband for decision-making. The working experience seems to give women more independence and self-assurance. It also provides them with an opportunity for wider human relationships, and an identity separate from that of being a widow. For many it was a means of keeping busy so they would have no time to look at their feelings. This escape sometimes delays their grief reaction till later. (Silverman, 1972) Some women, who had originally refused our help because they were too busy with their jobs, were grateful for contact with the aide later on when they had to face their feelings.

In what way did the helping network available to the widows influence their acceptance? We have information as to the availability of friends and family for all but 9%

of our population (3% of these being acceptances, and 6% being refusals). We only know three cases where no family was available (two of these cases being refusals). The greatest potential resource was the widow's own family, mostly-grown children (63.2%), siblings (48.9%), parents (22.1%). In about 40% of the cases, they had more than one generation of relatives to turn to. In 9.3% of the cases, the widow moved in with a relative, or had a relative move in with her.

We also inquired if the family had been found helpful. 82.3% mentioned the family as helpful immediately after the death, 52.9% found this help lasted beyond the first month or two of bereavement. 62% of our cases mentioned visiting of family as a fairly frequent occurrence. This percentage was much higher (85%) when we consider only those that accepted us. This would indicate that those with a close family relationship were the most open to help from our service.

The family relationship that seems to be the most helpful to a widow is that of grown children and grandchildren. The group of widows with grown children was the one with the lowest acceptance rate; only 47% accepted the aide. This would also explain the general drop in acceptance among the over-60 age group (see above). Later, when looking at the mode or excuse for refusals, we will see that 12% of all refusals came from a relative, mostly a grown child, who somewhat indignantly told the aide to leave his or her mother alone; that they were taking care of her. If the widow herself had been reached, the answer might have been different, but this seems to confirm the existing involvement of older widows with their grown children, even though they were often aware that they could not live their lives through their children and grandchildren and had to learn a certain independence for the relationship to remain good. Seen in light of a woman's life cycle, we observe here that the woman who is able to identify with the role of grandmother, adapts better to widowhood. It is a role which is not new to her, and which provides continuity of meaning to her life.

Other sources of help mentioned by the widows using our service were:

Friends:	39% found them helpful in the initial stages, and 28% reported that they continued to be helpful later on.
Doctor or clergy:	21.7% were helped by either or both in the initial stages, only 3.9% considered them still helpful later on. 14.3% mentioned clergy as helpful in the initial stages, 11% mentioned doctors.
Other widows:	6.9% mentioned them as helpful initially, 23.7% found them helpful later on. "Other widows" does not include the aide, but may include widows met through the service.

We can conclude, that except in a few exceptional cases, there was a natural helping network available. Oddly enough, this was true even more so among those who accepted us than those that refused. However, there may be real differences in the way this network functions, with certain lacks in effectiveness and a certain ambiguity about helping.

Although families were in many ways helpful, (especially, as we remarked earlier, when there were grown children) 16.3% of our cases mentioned that their family was also a problem, 6.0% being in conflict with their family over financial matters, such as relatives trying to borrow money or take advantage of them, 10.3% complaining of lack of understanding or indifference on the part of their family.

We have already indicated that the statistical information pointed to a quick waning interest of family and friends in the widow. This problem was frequently voiced at our widow's meetings. Family and friends rally round the widow at the time of death and shortly after, but soon lose patience and interest. A number of widows who initially refused us, or who accepted the aide although they felt they had no need for her because they were surrounded by family and friends at that time, later found that they were left very much to themselves and welcomed the opportunity of contact with the aide. They also perceived this contact as fulfilling a need that their family and friends, even if they continued showing interest, could not satisfy. Not only had the aide lived through the same experience, but she was a stranger, uninvolved in the home or neighborhood situation, which made it easier for the widows to unburden themselves. In the days of the extended family system, a new widow might well have found another widow in the family to relate to. At the present time this rarely occurs, but was usually mentioned as helpful when it did. Sometimes other widows at work or in the neighborhood took the initiative to reach out to the new widow. This came as a surprise but was much appreciated and considered very helpful.

The clergy or the doctor were two groups of people that the widows looked to naturally for help. We mentioned above that only 21% of our widows found them helpful initially, but like the family the interest of these professionals did not extend over a long time. If either doctor or clergyman had an extended contact with the widow, this often happened because there had been a personal friendship between them or the widow had been particularly active in the church.

The role of agencies is difficult to assess. When we had recourse to them we often found it difficult to obtain effective help, and many a widow was sent from one agency to another without obtaining satisfaction. We certainly do not know of all the cases that were receiving help from agencies, but in some cases that we were helping we knew that an agency was also involved meeting different needs of the widow or her family.

In seven families the problem centered around the children. At least three of them we knew had very definite psychological problems or had received help before the bereavement. The father's death brought their problem to crisis proportions and we helped the widow to turn to an agency.

Among the widows themselves three were drinking and had to be hospitalized. Four widows who received help had a past history of mental illness. One young widow whose husband had committed suicide also sought help as an outpatient for a while, although the aide had a fairly close relationship to her. It would seem that the aide could help at the level of the problem caused by widowhood itself, but that for problems existing before or extraneous to bereavement, which often became worse as a result of the husband's death, professional help had to be sought. This view is supported by the experience we had when a widow was referred to us by a psychiatrist who was making little progress with her. The aide who went to see her merely said, "She is bereaved." This was a problem the aide was competent to deal with, and little by little, she helped her to function again talking about those problems caused by her widowhood.

Initiating contact:

We would next like to describe the method used to initiate contact with the widows, how much effort was put into this reaching out, and what the results were.

The aide would normally proceed by sending a letter to the newly bereaved widow three to four weeks after the death, offering to visit her at a specified time, stating the reason for her visit and giving her phone number so the widow could refuse her or, if the time was inconvenient, set up another time. In only 22% of the cases was this letter directly followed by a visit as planned, and the widow found to be home. In 28% of the cases, the widow was not home and had not cancelled the appointment. If this happened, the aide would make some further effort by leaving a note, or telephoning, or repeating the visit. The high percentage of refusals despite the aide's effort indicates that in most cases the widow's absence was a manner of refusal. Since the aides found that much of their time would be wasted if they did not make sure the widow would be expecting them, they frequently called by phone on the morning the visit was planned, enquiring if the widow had received the letter, or asking for direction. In other cases, the widow took the initiative, calling to say she could not keep the appointment that day. This gave her the opportunity to find out more about the aide and the service, and gave the aide a chance to dispel suspicion and initiate a contact. This stage might lead to a firm refusal right away, to the visit as planned, to a new appointment, or to the beginning of a telephone relationship, with the widow not meeting the aide for quite a period of time. Such phone contacts, whether followed by a visit or not, occurred in 48% of the cases. In 2% of the cases the aide dropped by unannounced and was accepted. In these cases, the aide usually had had some previous connection with the new widow.

The data do seem to indicate that when the aide was able to appear in person to visit the widow, she had a greater chance of success. However, while a large percentage accepted through phone contacts, it must be kept in mind that some of these were initiated by the widows with the clear intention of refusing.

Follow up:

The contact between the widow and the aide was never intended to be a one-time effort. The aide always gave her home phone number, asking the widow to call her any time if she needed help or just wished to talk. She also offered to call back to find out how the widow was doing, or to keep her informed of any meetings which might be planned. In 68% of the cases where we were accepted, the relationship extended over at least a year. In the other cases, the aide would decide after a while that she was not needed any more, or that she had done what she could for the widow.

Further calling usually was at the aide's initiative. Although the widows were given the phone number, very few, 29% of the acceptance, took the initiative of calling the aide. However, many told us they had always kept the phone number on hand and that this had been a great comfort to them to know there was someone they could talk to. They did not call because they hesitated to bother the aide or lacked initiative in their depression. It did happen several times, however, that widows who thought they would never be interested in this sort of contact, became overcome by a sudden need to talk to someone, remembered the aide's card and called her, even in the middle of the night.

In some cases a closer relationship developed between the aides and the widows, leading to further visiting, joint outings and frequent phone conversations sometimes arising out of the particular need of the widow, sometimes merely out of a growing friendship between them.

We also organized meetings, giving the widows an opportunity to socialize and share their problems. This group contact was never intended to be the major emphasis of our service. Only 30% of those that accepted ever came to such meetings, and only 20% could be said to come with any regularity. The one-to-one relationship was the important one. Many widows did not care to belong to a group or were not emotionally ready to do so, but did appreciate greatly the individual relationship, where the aide did the reaching out. Our younger widows especially cared very little for the group meetings where they found themselves outnumbered by older women; however, in some cases the aide was successful in putting two young widows in touch with each other informally.

There were, on the other hand, some widows who seemed shy of the one-to-one relationship, and felt more at ease in the group. The meetings also provided a reason for keeping in touch, and gave some widows who had initially refused us the opportunity of changing their minds or finding out about the service at a later date.

Reasons for refusal:

Since this service was an experiment to reach out to a total population, offering them a new kind of help, it seems worthwhile to look further at the reasons given for refusing the aide. First we will look at the reasons given at the time when the aide initially tried to reach the widows, shortly after the bereavement. Secondly, we will examine the results of interviews with those who had refused us, and see if after a lapse of time and the fact that our service became better known, their attitude had changed about the helpfulness of such a service.

When looking at the reasons for refusal at the time of initial contact, it is important to keep in mind that many widows were quite suspicious of being approached by a stranger. Dorchester is an area where there is legitimate reason for such fear. In addition, many widows were particularly fearful living without a man in the house. Several acquired a dog. One told us that she kept a heavy tool within reach when she went to sleep, as a possible weapon. We were aware of initial hostility or suspicion in at least 21% of the cases. Some widows, we found out afterwards, had taken precautions for the time of the visit, such as having someone of the family present at the time, or arranging to be called or visited by a friend when the aide's visit was under way. Some had checked with their local priest to find out if we were legitimate. It is therefore quite possible that a number of refusals were really motivated by fear, although other excuses were given.

The reasons or modes of refusal were the following:

—too busy with job, family, setting affairs in order   28.6%
—plenty of support from friends and family   25.3%
—family (usually grown child) refusing calls   12.1%
—independent, no need for support   12.1%
—no response to any of the aide's efforts to contact   7.7%
—will not open the door   7.7%
—seems to accept first contact, but refuses because
   no need   6.5%

_____

100%

The last group above seemed to accept a visit or had a lengthy phone call with the aide. They showed some interest in the service, but later let the aide know that they had no need for her help. In contrast to this group, and in addition to the 91 total refusals, 13% of our acceptances (18 widows) refused us at first, then changed their minds within the first year and were glad to receive our help. Our timing may have been wrong and some widows should have been contacted later. There can be no hard and fast rules for everyone in this matter. The important factor seems to be availability over a period of time. Some of these widows were still too much in shock, or were too involved with material decisions following the death, and had not yet felt the need to talk to another widow. We also mentioned earlier other reasons why some would not feel loss and loneliness right away such as work or the group whose family refused on their behalf.

To find out more about those who had refused our initial contact, we interviewed them one or two years later. Of these 91 widows, 2 were remarried and not available to be

interviewed, 27 had moved, 22 formally refused to be interviewed, while 5 successfully avoided the interviewer. We
therefore were able to question 35 widows (38% of the
refusals) to find out what had been their reaction when
first contacted. Would they have had a different answer if
they had understood better what the service was about,
how had they made out, and had they at some later date
wished for the kind of help the aide might have been able
to provide?

The following table indicates the kinds of response received:

Independent, not the sort of thing for her, not use-ful to talk to a stranger . . . keeps to herself	42.9%
Would still refuse the aide because of enough fam-ily support	22.8%
Might have accepted if contacted later	11.4%
Might have accepted if understood better what it was about	8.6%
Joined the service later of their own accord	8.6%
Remained hostile	5.7%
	100%

It is not possible to draw any conclusions by comparing
these responses to the reasons for refusal at initial contact
since the 35 women we were able to interview would not be
representative of each group of refusals, nor was it worthwhile with such small numbers to identify what happened
in each category at a later date. The importance of the
above table is in showing us that 28.6 of those interviewed
might have been receptive to our help at some later date
or if we had been able to explain our service better to
them.

Content of the relationship:

In this section, we would like to examine how the **aide** developed a relationship to the widow, what kind of problems they discussed, what kind of help the aide was able to provide. For this information we will turn most to the data provided by the aides themselves in the course of their work, to information gained from the widows at meetings and discussions, and from in-depth follow-up interviews of the widows we served.

Two areas of conversation were found to provide basis for opening contacts with a new widow: talking of her children, and making sure the widow was aware of all the material benefits to which she might be entitled. Once the ice was broken, it became easier to talk of the death event and about the widow herself. How did she look upon her new situation? What feelings did she have about the deceased and his death? How helpful and understanding did she find friends and family? The aide usually found it helpful to mention some of her own experiences and feelings as a new widow.

The problems brought up in the course of the relationship were the following, in order of frequency, expressed in percentages of the total of acceptances:

Need of the widow to talk, to experience companionship and friendship with the aide, to share her experience   81.4%

Problems related to housing—mostly because of the bad neighborhood, lodging considered inadequate, or because of a wish to move closer to relatives   34%

Problems related to children   28%

Need for assurance that she would successfully weather the crisis   25%

Inadequate income	24%
Problems in relationships to family or relatives, meeting with lack of understanding	23%
Wish to get a job or training for a job	22%
Financial problems related to claims for benefits	19%

The aides made a great effort to inform themselves about such things as claims, benefits, social services available, and often were able to give assistance or advice to the widows in their material concerns. It is clear, however, that the greatest need did not arise out of material hardship. What the widows most appreciated was the opportunity to talk, to let out their feelings, and discuss their own emotional needs with the aide, finding in the relationship a special quality because of the shared experience.

As we saw earlier, although most widows had family available, those who accepted our service either did not find family helpful or found that talking with the aide met other needs. We can illustrate this from our in-depth interviews. A young widow whose husband had died suddenly in an accident found that she had to go over and over the death event. Her family would not listen to her. When the aide came:

> "She told me how her husband had died. It was such a relief to be able to tell her how mine had died also."

Another said:

> "The aide could understand that I can't eat, I can't sleep, because she has lived through the same thing."

Frequently these young widows told us of the relief experienced in being able to talk freely to the aide about their feelings. Family, friends, people around them expected them either to stop grieving and remarry, or wished to see them devote themselves to their children and accept the "fact" that their own life was finished. Another area that young widows sometimes liked to discuss after they began to know the aide was the problem of meeting men again, how to handle dating. Going out as a widow is a different experience from going out as a young single girl. Their own feelings are very different and the expectations of men often difficult to handle.

The sincerity of the aide came through, beyond social differences. One widow was very conscious of social class, being herself uneducated and quickly worried about people looking down on her or pitying her. She said,

> I could not have accepted a lady bountiful, but I felt the aide was sincere. When she would call me, I thought we would chit-chat for a while, but in no time I found myself spilling out all my problems. When I put the phone down, I felt so much better.

A widow over 50 years old, extremely involved with children and grandchildren, almost in a matriarchal way, said to us,

> I could not show my family how I felt although we are very close. I could talk to my mother when she was living, because she was widowed. I could talk to the aide because she is widowed. When my mother died, I had to call the aide. There was no one else I could really talk to. She helped me a lot. I don't feel I can burden my children with how I feel.

Her mother had had a mental breakdown when she became widowed. She felt the same might have happened to her if she had not had this opportunity of talking to the aide and her mother.

A young widow when first seen by the aide started out appearing very brave, very strong in her faith, quite certain she was going to be able to face things. The aide was full of admiration for her but also told her it might get worse before it would get better. In fact, four months later this widow had an enormous need to let out her feelings and saw herself as falling apart. She was much helped by a priest who was a close friend and helped her grieve. "But," she said, "the aide's help was different because she had been there. She knew the pain. She had told me what to expect."

The aide is frequently called upon to reassure the widow that she can pull through, and here, her own example is useful. Sometimes the widow gets so frightened of her own feelings that she worries she may be going crazy. The aide is able to say to her, "You're not going crazy, I felt the same way." With the aide, the widow feels she can own up to all her feelings and her fears.

The aide also encouraged the widow to go out, to indulge herself a little, to get out of a rut. She offered her companionship in her loneliness. One extreme case of this was an older woman living in a very bad area of Dorchester, who had no friends, no relatives. She told the interviewer later on, "I was just about ready to lie down and die. When the aide came it was like a piece of heaven."

Apart from help for themselves, widows with children often were eager to share with the aide their concern for their children. Through our experience in the Widow-to-Widow program we have come to ask ourselves if children, even more than their mothers, are not the real casualty of bereavement. The child's adjustment is very much dependent on the kind of reaction the mother has to her bereavement and how she communicates with her children at that time. We served 62 widows with children under 16. 36 of these noticed in their children a marked change in behavior either at school, where the quality of their work would go down, or at home in their relationship to their family or peers. 39 children showed themselves to be extremely disturbed by the death of the father, in some cases to the extent of requiring professional help. At meetings, or privately with the aide, widows would raise such questions as, "Should I let my child see my sorrow?" "How do I cope with my child's grief when I am under so much strain because of my own sorrow?" "How do I deal with the antagonism which is developing between me and my child about the relationship we each had to his father?" Sharing these questions with the aide and other widows relieved them of some of their anxiety and helped them gain perspective on their problem, especially if the aide or other widows had met with a similar difficulty.

In all these cases the aide did not try to act as a professional. The help she offered always drew its unique quality from the shared experience.

Chapter IV

THE WIDOWED SERVICE LINE

By Elizabeth Wilson

In January, 1970, we faced a very painful decision: What would we do if we had no money to continue into the next year? Our funds ran out in the summer of 1970. To continue as an outreach program would be unfair to the many new people we might meet just as we had to close up shop.

We tried very hard to find people in Dorchester who might continue the service on a volunteer basis. We weren't sure ourselves how much we could continue to provide back up and give direction as volunteers, either. None of the people we served were ready to take on this responsibility. They wanted to help, but to run a program for a community of 250,000 people seemed overwhelming. In addition, the thought of reaching out to people they did not know was intimidating. While they could agree that they appreciated the visit, they could not easily see themselves doing this.

We are still hoping that something can be organized on a parish basis in cooperation with the clergy. Volunteers can only run a Widow-to-Widow program in a small community, the size of a congregation or a parish.

We were also sure that it was not a good idea to reach out unless you could stay with the person over an extended period of time. We had to consider how to phase out the program and, at the same time, if we received a budget (we had applied for some funds from the National Institute of Mental Health), we had to decide what would be the best way to use this money.

We decided not to simply continue as we had been before. We wanted to explore other methods of giving service that would reach a wider geographic area and that would make it possible to serve widowers as well.

As a result of our experience in the Widow-to-Widow program, we knew that we had to use other widows in any service we set up. We also found that we had a number of inquiries about our work as a result of newspaper articles and as a result of our appearance on T.V. We were able to help these people on the telephone without a personal contact; this was also true in the Widow-to-Widow Program. Many widows worked or, for other reasons, preferred to talk with us on the phone. The idea of "hot lines" for every other kind of problem was all around us, and we decided this idea might be worth trying for the widowed as well. The cost of running this kind of an operation for an entire community would be minimal and it would be possible to help many more people, including widowers. It also became evident there were widowed people out there who were interested in volunteering their time and energies.

We knew in late June we would receive the grant. We spent the summer planning and, in October, we started recruiting volunteer help. Twenty men and women agreed to donate a definite time during the week when they would be available to make return calls.

We thought the service should be available twenty-four hours a day, seven days a week. To supply this, on the basis of our own office staff and phone service, would have called for more funds and manpower than we had available, so we decided to use an answering service. This also pretty much eliminated crank calls, since these callers usually don't wish to leave a phone number and name.

The calls were picked up twice a day by Dorothy Mac-Kenzie, or myself. We were the coordinators of the line and we fed the calls out to the volunteers according to their schedule. We were available for any difficulties the volunteers encountered and, also, to offer advice and support.

Meetings of the volunteers and coordinators were held on the second and fourth Thursdays of each month to exchange ideas, talk over problems of the callers and, generally, learn something about how we could give better service. The volunteers made the calls from their own homes; the coordinators, also, did most of their work at home.

The kind of calls we received ran the gamut from lonely people who just wanted someone to talk to, to people who needed some very practical advice about what benefits were available to them: how did they go about getting these benefits; where could they find a housekeeper; job training possibilities; and what social organizations were there just for widowed people? In some instances, the callers were severely depressed, even to the point of considering suicide; others had become alcoholics. Dorothy and I were usually very closely involved in these situations and, where possible, tried to mobilize community resources to make a referral.

By and large, most calls were made by people who were lonely, feeling isolated or misunderstood, and who really wanted to know how they could better their situation. One of the most valuable services I think we performed was putting people in touch with other widowed people either in their own area or in similar circumstances. We were most helpful in this respect to the young widows with babies, some with one yet to be born.

We received calls from two young, pregnant widows, and, from one or two who had had children shortly after the death of their husband. We had a meeting of these young women, which gave them an opportunity to voice their very real concern about how to handle their feelings about, among other things: how to say "I am a widow," how to be able to cope with the astonished horror of others, and how to start dating again. I feel they will be meeting again from time to time and they turn to each other now instead of to us. Most people feel better, at least for a time, with someone "in the same boat" and, often they team up to go to meetings, shopping, and so forth.

Some calls led to ongoing relationships with the volunteers, because they became friends or because the problem was such that the volunteer should remain available.

Most important was the fact that some people called to volunteer. We tried to meet people, and invite them to an orientation meeting.

One of the volunteers on our line was Arthur Churchill, also President of Eschaton—a widowed group in Boston.

A Volunteer's Viewpoint—Arthur Churchill

I have been a volunteer on the Widowed Service Line since it started, and it has been most interesting and rewarding.

I have been widowed almost three years and I know what it is like to raise a large family alone. I have seven children. I am also the President of Eschaton, a club for the widowed. In fact, it was through this club that I became a volunteer.

After my wife died, I knew I had to make a new life, and this is partly why I became involved. I also like people and enjoy meeting them. I do not claim to be any kind of professional in any sense. I try to relate not only what I have found out from the coordinators and the volunteer meetings but, also, from my own experience. We try to give the information needed or get it if not immediately available. We let the caller know we will try to get it and call him back. I've found that on the second call, people are most often more receptive. Loneliness is the most frequent reason given for calls. As President of the Eschaton Club, I have had the pleasure of meeting many of these people whom we invite to our meetings.

I have had a few disappointing calls, and some people just call out of curiosity. I firmly believe the widowed can best help each other because we know the loneliness and grief involved. I am quite sure this is why we have done so well in this program.

DISCUSSION NOTES:

Discussion centered around how the Line was advertised and who it reached. There was concern that the most isolated people might not hear about the program while they were the ones who might need it most. It is impossible to know who is reached by advertisements on radio, T.V. and in the newspapers. These are usually public service notices the stations broadcast at various times during the day and night to reach different segments of the population who are listening at these various times. The Line was also announced in church and temple bulletins. There are at least two kinds of people: those who can be reached by publicity and those who can be reached only by the one-to-one process on an outreach basis. One of the participants reported on what she is doing in her community since she first heard about this workshop:

I have become more aware of people around me. I now read all the obituaries in the local paper and send a note to each newly bereaved widow. I write a letter, saying: 'I can't help you now, but I am available if you want to call me later on.' If they do not call, I call them back. We have to reach out systematically to the newly bereaved; otherwise, we will not reach them. Sometimes they call me and we talk on the telephone. It gives them an opportunity to keep airing their problems—not necessarily solving them. They can keep gnawing at the problem until they evolve their own solution.

Chapter V

WHO THE WIDOWED SERVICE LINE SERVED

By Ruby Abrahams

The telephone service model can answer the needs of widowed people who will take the initiative to call in for help. At present, we do not know who among the widowed respond, and who do not respond to the Service Line. Probably, the very newly bereaved, and the widowed in poverty areas, are unlikely to call in even though they may need help. For these groups, an outreach program may be more effective. The Widowed Service Line, an outgrowth of the Widow-to-Widow Program was an attempt to expand the service to a wider community. This chapter analyzes some of the characteristics and problems of those who did contact the Line, and describes briefly the volunteers' handling of these calls.

In the first seven months of operation, 750 people called the Widowed Service Line. These calls were received from a wide geographic area in and around Boston. The callers heard about the Line in a variety of ways, television being the most effective means of publicity. Of all callers to the Line, 54% heard about it on T.V., 12% from local newspapers, 10% from church bulletins, 9% from the radio, 7% through a friend, 6% from the metropolitan newspaper and 2% were referred by professionals. At the peak of the television coverage, during the first three months of operation, calls averaged 60 per week. After the Line became better known in the community, more referrals were received from professionals such as clergy and social workers, who felt unable to help with the specific emotional problems of the widowed.

Callers' Age and Duration of Widowhood:

When a Widowed Service Line is thus publicized in a metropolitan area, who calls in? Of all callers, 90% were women. The age breakdown is as follows: (There was no significant difference in the ages of male and female callers) :—

Age	
Under 40 years	12%
41-50 years	22%
51-60 years	36%
61 plus years	30% (N-521)

Ages of callers ranged from twenty-four to ninety years, but the most typical caller was a woman in her fifties.

Is it the newly bereaved, or those with longer term residual problems of widowhood who have reached out to use this service?

Widowed less than 1 year	30%
Widowed 1 to 2 years	16%
Widowed 3 to 6 years	23%
Widowed 7 plus years	31% (N=470)

Almost half (46%) were widowed within the last two years, and are at the stage of handling the earlier problems of grief, disengagement from their previous life style, and the early stages of meeting the need to re-engage in new roles and relationships. A smaller proportion widowed 3 to 6 years (23%), are still trying to adjust and develop a new life style. One-third of the callers were

58

those still unadjusted after seven years of widowhood. There was no significant difference in duration of widowhood between male and female callers.

Types of Problems Presented by Callers at Different Stages of Widowhood:

Caller's requests were categorized as follows:

1) Lonely—required a listener   20%

2) Lonely—wants to meet people   37%

3) Requires specific information:

    a) Financial   6%
    b) Employment or training   4%
    c) Other (Includes information for handicapped people, housing and legal problems, professional care for self or children, health facilities, housekeepers, child care)   12%

4) Requests information about the Line 16% (most of these were later placed in categories 1 or 2)

5) Offers services as volunteer   5% (N=567)

Categories 1, 2, and 4 together (in which loneliness and isolation are the main problems) account for 73% of all needs expressed by callers. Of those who wanted information specifically on how to meet new people and expand their social relationships network:

   58% were interested in social clubs for the widowed.
   30% requested contact with another widowed person living in their own area.

12% asked specifically how to meet members of the opposite sex.

The three main categories of callers' needs:
1) For a listener
2) To meet people
3) For specific practical information

were found to be significantly related to their stage of widowhood. The widowed who call within the first year of their bereavement are most likely to need an understanding listener. In the sequence of transitions after bereavement, they are in the phase of "impact" or "recoil" when the individual experiences a period of turmoil as he begins to realize the full effects of his changed life situation.

Callers who are widowed from approximately two to six years are most likely to be in the "recovery" stage. They are beginning to develop new roles and relationships and look for ways to re-engage in the social system. These callers were more likely to request information about how to make new contacts and where to go to meet people and develop new friendships.

Among callers who were widowed a longer time (7 years or more), there were still requests for information about meeting people but a higher proportion of these long term widowed people had specific requests about financial, legal, housing, and employment problems. This may reflect another critical stage for the older widowed person, when the children have grown up and leave home. The widow or widower is then faced with living alone for the first time. At this stage there may be questions about sharing housing accommodations that are too large, or moving into a smaller dwelling unit. The older person, as he approaches the age for claiming Social Security may also need help with financial problems. The indications are that the widowed person who does not successfully build a new life style after some years of widowhood, who may have depended too heavily on family or work for meaningful self-definition, may be in difficulties again when the family disperses or retirement age is reached.

Types of Problems Presented by Different Age Groups:

The younger caller, under 45, is most likely to present problems other than social. 83% of these younger callers had children under 16 at home and many of the problems they discussed with volunteers concerned their children and the problems of the single parent. At the stage of raising young children, the widowed seem to have less need of help in making new friendships. This may be partially because the close relationships with children are emotionally sustaining and they feel less need to seek new relationships, or it may be that children themselves bring the parent into social networks in connection with the child's activities. Additionally, there are more opportunities and facilities available for young people to meet others with whom they can develop close relationships. These younger callers were more likely to ask for information on specific practical problems, or they needed a listener for their emotional problems. The latter applies especially to the more recently bereaved. Callers in the 45-60 range are more likely to need help in finding ways of rebuilding their lives, in making new friendships and finding new satisfying roles for themselves as widowed and single people. The older caller, over 60, is more like the younger caller in that she more often requested information about practical problems or an understanding listener to help with his or her feelings and frustrations.

Type of Household as a Determinant of Need:

Who is more likely to seek help from the Widowed Service Line, widowed people living alone, or living with others?

According to household, the callers were categorized as follows:

Living alone	49%
Living with children under 16	30%
Living with children over 16	14%
Living with other relatives or friend	7% (N=458)

If the type of household tells us anything about the need for help, first the widowed living alone and, secondly, those with younger children are the most likely to seek help. It was also found in the Widow-to-Widow Program that women with younger children at home were more likely to accept help early after the loss of the spouse. The responsibility of raising children alone, plus the fact that the needs of children themselves increase immediately after the death, place a heavy burden on the widow struggling with her own grief.

Both younger and older callers who sought help from the telephone service within the first two years of widowhood were more likely to be either living alone or with young children. Therefore, regardless of age, these two groups seem to experience the most immediate pressures and tensions after loss of the spouse and these pressures increase the likelihood of response to a publicized service for the widowed.

Employment and Loneliness:

Many widowed people find that it is helpful to take a job, or return to work, as soon as they have recovered from the immediate impact of the death. The work situation involves roles and identities which are outside of the marriage situation. The individual can carry on in these roles, or even lose himself in these roles, which are not involved in the stress and turmoil of his bereavement.

Were the employed callers less likely to feel loneliness than those not employed? Our data suggest that this is not so. Callers who were employed full-time were the most likely to ask for help in making new friendships. This holds for all age groups and it is suggested that, although having a job may alleviate the distress of bereavement, relationships made in the work situation are no substitute for the intimacy sought in new friendships.

A large majority of the callers to the Widowed Service Line were not employed. Percentages are as follows:

Employed full-time	27%
Employed part-time	12%
Not employed	61% (N=478)

Since most of the callers responded as a result of T.V. publicity, these figures may reflect the greater exposure to the media of women who are at home all day. However, the T.V. announcements often appeared during the evening hours and other sources of information were available. The indications are that women who are at home all day are **more** oppressed by the stresses of widowhood than those who work and therefore are more likely to seek help from a service for the widowed. The work situation, however, does not provide the social intimacy necessary for a healthy recovery after disengagement from previous roles and relationships. Employment may even, to some extent, help the widowed to escape from facing the realities of their social isolation.

The Widower:

The number of widowers served by the Widow Service Line was relatively small. Our data indicate that there was little age difference between widow and widower callers. Differences in duration of widowhood were very slight. The widowers covered the range from those in the stages of early bereavement to those unadjusted after seven years. The differences are small, but it is possible that the men were somewhat more likely than the women to seek help earlier, within the first few months after the death of the spouse.

Male callers (55%) were slightly more likely than female callers (48%) to be living alone, and the proportions were identical for widows and widowers calling the line who had children at home (44%). As with the widow, the widower, living alone or left with young children, is especially in need of help and is most likely to respond to the Widowed Service Line.

Differences again were slight in the categories of problems presented by widows and widowers. Widowers (41%) were somewhat more likely than widows (35%) to ask how to meet new friends and somewhat less likely to ask for practical information (widowers 37%, widows 46%). The men were less likely than the women to mask their problems with a general inquiry asking what the Line was about, they seemed to have less hesitation stating their problems directly. Widower callers usually were answered by widower volunteers, although as our experience with the Line developed, we found that many of the widowers preferred to talk to the female volunteers and often were more expressive of their emotional problems when talking to a woman. Some of the women also preferred to talk to widowers, especially about specific practical problems, such as finance, housing, and legal matters. The option of talking to a widow or widower can be given to the caller.

The question most often presented by the widower with young children at home is how to find a housekeeper, or full-time baby sitter. This is a pressing problem and for the widower with limited means, it is hard to find a solution. In one or two cases the volunteer was able to refer a widow who called the Line asking for this kind of work, but the need is largely unmet. To solve the problem, very often the widower is considering remarriage. Within the overall program, discussion with clergymen and others who are involved with social groups for the widowed has indicated that there is an urgent need for "remarriage counseling" among the widowed. Few services of this kind are offered and the pressures, especially for the widower with children, can often result in an unfortunate second marriage.

Loneliness And Isolation Of The Widowed:

Our data indicates that those who called the Widowed Service Line are mainly people suffering from loneliness and isolation. Volunteers asked callers about their social life and categorized them as follows:

Active social life	22%	
Isolated	61%	
Bereaved too recently	17%	(N=455)

If active, their relationships involved:

Friends	43%
Clubs	34%
Church	18%
Relatives	5% (N—99)

Thus among the callers who had found some new satis-factory social relationships, the majority were helped in this by their friends and a considerable number had been helped by joining clubs.

In response to the question, "Who has helped you most with your grief and adjustment problems," callers in-dicated they were helped by:

Relatives	46%
Friends	22%
Clergy	3%
Other professionals	4%
Participation in organizations	4%
No one	21% (N=257)

First, relatives and, secondly, friends, seem to have been the most helpful in the earlier stages of grief and re-adjustment. Professionals, especially clergy who seem to be in a strategic position to help the widowed, have appar-ently offered little assistance. The data suggests that for most people, relatives are helpful in the early stages of bereavement, but the callers who found satisfactory rela-tionships later on, found them among friends or at clubs for the widowed. It is possible that widowed people who continue to live in a close family network and find satis-faction in kin relationships do not need outside help and are not likely to contact a service for the widowed.

Who the Widowed Service Line Served

Financial Situation of Callers:

Callers to the Widowed Service Line did not mention financial problems as a major issue. From the records their financial situation was categorized as follows:

1) Well off   3%
2) Adequate   33%
3) Tight   16%
4) Hardship   4%
5) No financial problem
    recorded   45% (N=538)

This in part reflects the fact that a telephone service does not reach the financially disadvantaged. Although the Line was publicized in the local newspapers and on the radio stations for the low income, inner city area, we received few calls from that community. To reach the widowed in the poor areas and the black community would require an outreach program.

Many callers were given additional information about financial benefits, but this rarely was the problem for which they called the Line.

The Volunteers:

The Widowed Service Line was operated by a team of 18 volunteers (13 widows and 5 widowers). With two exceptions, these volunteers were all in full-time jobs and had children to care for. They were almost all in the 40's and 50's, with no more than high school education. They were recruited in various ways. Two had been helped in the Widow-to-Widow outreach program and moved into helping roles when this new phase of the program opened. Others heard about the program through the media and offered their services. Some heard about it from friends, who were already accepted as volunteers. Most of those who dropped out were in this last category. Commitment is more likely when the motivation to join is independent and self-initiated.

In selecting volunteers the following characteristics were important:

1) That they were recovered enough from their own bereavement and making a satisfactory adjustment to their widowhood.

2) That they could talk about it.

3) That they really wanted to help others and had already done some reaching out to widowed friends of their own.

4) That they had enough commitment to give the necessary time for calls and regularly attending the bi-monthly volunteers' meetings.

Styles of Caregiving:

Observation of this group of volunteers has indicated that the mutual helping concept involves a fluid, fast moving, dynamic situation, in which the needs of helpers, as well as those seeking help, are being met. The helpers enter the volunteer group at different stages in their own adjustment process. Their needs and their life situation affect their style of caregiving.

Caregiving styles range from a style similar to the professional/client type of relationship at one extreme to a friendship type of relationship at the other extreme. The professional/client relationship implies some distance between the helper and the one being helped, where the helper

feels more knowledgeable and informed about the adjustment process and wishes to pass on this information to the
seeker of help; the friendship relationship implies that the
helper and the one seeking help are sharing equally their
feelings and experience. Between these two extremes, there
is a range of helping relationships, in which varying needs
at different levels are being met on both sides of the helping relationship.

Some volunteers tended to focus on finding opportunities
for callers to move out, get involved, develop skills, feel
needed. They were resourceful and innovative in finding
the appropriate outlets in the caller's own community and
successful in persuading the callers to get involved in these
activities. Other volunteers also suggested resources, but
put more emphasis on listening to "feelings and frustrations." These volunteers preferred to work more inten-
sively with fewer callers, whereas the former type of helper
would carry a heavier load. Yet another focus of the mutual helping relationship was developed by those volunteers
who sought a friendship relationship with their callers,
where emotional inputs were equally exchanged in the helping process. These volunteers had frequent contact with
some of their callers, sometimes meeting them, going out
with them, or inviting them to their home. In some cases
these volunteers were themselves helped dramatically by
their involvement in the mutual-help program.

These different modes of helping have all been effective.
If there were any way of sorting out the callers, so that
the most appropriate volunteer could be assigned to each
caller, it might be possible to maximize the volunteers' helping capacities as a whole. No method was found for achiev-
ing this on the Widowed Service Line. However, given a
clearer understanding of what is involved in the mutual

helping process, it may be possible to devise such a sorting procedure in other programs. Further research and consideration of the different modes of helping encountered in the mutual-help process has many implications at the program level for those who are setting up and administering mutual-help groups.

Follow-up:

The volunteers felt that most of their callers could be adequately dealt with in two or three telephone conversations. In the telephone encounter, the stage of unloading feelings and getting into the deeper feeling levels of the callers' problems may be reached in the first or the second conversation. One or two further supportive calls were often sufficient to help the caller over a bad spell or to give her/him the necessary push to move out and start getting involved with new friends and activities. The volunteers all said that they continued making calls as long as they felt the caller needed them and it was always left open for the caller to call back if he or she wished. Most of the volunteers were following up extensively over a longer period (3 or 4 months), at least two of their callers.

Spin-Offs from the Widowed Service Line:

A major function of the telephone service model is that it provides a 24-hour-a-day, 7-days-a-week answering service. The call is returned by a widowed volunteer within 24 hours. Another widow or widower volunteer is able to help because he or she has been through these same feelings and eventually has found solutions.

A second function of the telephone service program is in making contact between widowed people who live in the same neighborhood. Sometimes the lonely caller was glad to be given the name of one or two other widowed people living close by. The widowed people might become telephone friends, or they might meet and go out together. Alternatively, if there were a sufficient number of widowed callers within one community, who were interested in developing a local mutual-help program, this could be encouraged and supported. The nuclei of a number of such "spin-off" programs in different areas have developed from the Widowed Service Line.

A third function of the telephone service is to effect an exchange of needs and offerings. For example, a number of widowed people have homes which are too large and they may offer accommodations to another widowed person who wishes to move and does not want to live alone. Some widows offered housekeeping or child care services and there were requests for these services especially from widowers with young children.

Organization, Volunteer Turnover and New Opportunities:

A mutual-help program involves a dynamic, fluid process which benefits the helper as well as the seeker of help. Some of the volunteers, after a few months in the program, developed their self-confidence and outreach skills so that they were ready to move into new and different activities. Some of these volunteers leave the program. Others may stay with the program but wish to move into new roles or levels of responsibility. On the other hand, some of the callers who seek help for themselves, may in turn wish to move into the helping role. On the Widowed Service Line a number of callers who were helped did eventually volunteer their services.

It is essential to keep the organization flexible enough to accommodate this ongoing, fluid process of development as it becomes appropriate for the helpers and the seekers of help to move into new roles and relationships in order to further their own self-growth. The two coordinators of the Widowed Service Line originally were aides in the Widow-to-Widow outreach program. During the three and a half years this program was operating, these widows developed a high level of helping skills. On the Widowed Service Line, very disturbed, extremely depressed, or suicidal callers were referred to either of the two coordinators, who successfully handled these difficult, sometimes emergency level cases. This often involved staying on the Line for two or three hours with the caller, and frequently this was late at night. These skillful helpers have been able to help other widowed people through severe crises and moments of stress. They also have now moved into roles involving coordinating, supervising, training and developing new "spin-off" programs.

Helping skills develop out of the mutual experience of widowhood. The volunteers helped each other to develop these skills further by mutual discussion and exchange of experiences at bimonthly volunteers' meetings. These discussions were guided by the two coordinators who shared their own experiences with the volunteers.

A professional "consultant" can be helpful in clarifying perspectives and conceptualizing insights for the volunteer. To aid the self-growth of the volunteers, the professional may add his/her skills in collaboration with, but not in control of, the non-professional caregiver. For maximum self-growth, the volunteers should run their own program.

PART II

How to Help Each Other

Introduction

This section contains information needed to set up a program for the widowed in a community.

In Chapter VI, Phyllis Silverman outlines the steps which individuals who want to set up a program for the widowed might follow. Many already existing groups for the widowed were represented at the workshop. To ensure that all would benefit from the varied experiences of these organizations and become aware of the many kinds of programs in existence, a representative of each group was asked to give a formal presentation about his organization. These presentations make up Chapter VII, and provide a sense of the various organizational and programmatic problems these groups faced.

Following these presentations, the participants joined one of five workshops. Every group included a member of an existing organization for the widowed, a staff member from the Widow-to-Widow program, and people from both rural and urban communities. These workshops, extending over a six-hour period, gave individuals an opportunity to talk about what was needed to develop a program in their town. The content of these discussions is summarized in Chapter VIII. In these discussions, everyone had an opportunity to express some of their inner feelings about what a widowed person must cope with, and how these feelings affect his or her ability to help others. The value of mutual help is reviewed and steps in developing a possible program are carefully detailed.

In Chapter IX Phyllis Silverman discusses her role as a mental health professional working with a mutual help program. She cautions against allowing professionals to direct such programs because often the mutual help is sacrificed to what the professionals feel the widowed need. Chapter X contains a description of an orientation program for new volunteers. To enable the volunteer to apply his unique expertise to the task of helping other widowed people, training, in the professional sense, should be minimized. The word "orientation" was chosen to imply a preparation, not training process.

Finally, the Epilogue is a summary of the all too brief closing discussion of the workshop. The frankness with which people talked about their feelings was made possible by a week-end in which people became friends. They talked of the need of widowed people to share their experiences and feelings with each other, and the success of this method for learning to cope more effectively. The problems of loneliness were very real, and it was suggested that one way of alleviating this was to help others in similar difficulty.

Chapter VI

ISSUES TO CONSIDER IN SETTING UP
OUTREACH PROGRAMS

By Phyllis Silverman, Ph.D.

In developing any new program or service there are certain procedures which should be followed. It takes more than personal charisma and initiative to reach the goal of developing a program for the widowed in any given community. There seems to be an orderly progression of activities that bring the hoped-for end result. Even so, I've come to believe, not necessarily in a mystical way, that everything has a time. An idea may develop, people become interested, allies are recruited, a momentum begins and then the pieces begin to fall together so that the idea (sometimes almost suddenly) becomes a reality. This can take a year or more. Therefore I do not envision that anyone reading this will instantly, by following the recommended formulae, develop a program or service for the widowed.

The time span between conception and actualization in the Widow-to-Widow program will give an example of my meaning. I began the research that led to this program in October, 1964. I crystallized the idea of a Widow-to-Widow program approximately one year later in 1965. It took me two years working at it on a part-time basis to do the preliminary work before the program finally began in May, 1967.

I was ready to abandon the idea by the winter of 1966-67. It was not easy to find widowed people who wanted to

75

work in an outreach program, and it was more difficult to find money to support the program on a demonstration basis. We were willing to begin if we had at least three women to reach out. For a period of at least 6 months everyone approached was not interested . . . and then I met Dorothy MacKenzie. She was the catalyst, and within a month Mary Pettipas and Carrie Wynn joined us. Things began to move, and the National Funeral Directors Association and the Massachusetts Funeral Directors Association agreed to provide us with sufficient money to start.

In looking at the steps to follow in initiating a program, it is important to consider who the individual is who is trying to do this. To some extent, what happens depends on the individual's background, experience, and links to the community. In the instance of the Widow-to-Widow program, I was the prime mover. I am a social worker, with a Ph.D. and a good deal of experience in the mental health field. I had no roots in the community in which we worked. In fact, I was not even widowed. I was a newly-wed when this program began. Much of what I did initially was because I had a job to do and I was told I could try whatever made sense to me. However, it was still a job; I did not do it out of personal mission or need. Therefore, I started at a different point from any widowed person who had such a personal commitment and need, and who lived in the community he wanted to serve. In the same way a widowed individual with a good deal of organizational experience, or who is very involved in his community, will approach the problem differently from the widowed individual who has done none of these things. While the sequence of events leading to attaining a goal may differ, lack of experience should never deter someone from acting to develop the kind of mutual help program referred to here.

Issues to Consider in Setting up Outreach Programs

In presenting the following steps, I want to note that these are not necessarily to be followed in sequential order. Sometimes things occur simultaneously, and in many instances depend on opportunity.

Issues to Consider:

The first step, as in any program, is to establish goals. What are the possibilities: Outreach, Hot Line, discussion groups, social clubs? When the widowed are considered, this includes not only helping people who are widowed, but also helping newly-bereaved men and women, who, though now widowed still feel married, socially and emotionally. These are people who are raw, tender, fearful, and for the most part, incapable of reaching out to ask for help. Thus, it becomes not only a program of reaching a population of people who are widowed, but also of involving these very sensitive people in a program.

Programs will vary depending on which stage of widowhood becomes the focus. The Widow-to-Widow program tried to reach newly bereaved. Unless they reached all in the community under sixty, they might have missed many who needed them most. (Age, too, makes a big difference; the elderly who are widowed are, in a way, a different population with different needs from those who are younger when their spouse dies. This does not mean they would not benefit from an outreach program.) To reach everyone, as in this case, a method had to be found of identifying the bereaved soon after they become widowed. Thus, it was useful to ask the Bureau of Vital Statistics for Death Certificates which are a matter of public record. Clergy and funeral directors are also useful as they are in contact with almost everyone who dies in a given community. When working in a particular parish or synagogue, few people would go unnoticed if the clergy reported each death to the program and told the family about the service.

After establishing goals and methods, it is necessary to see what kind of workers or volunteers are needed to achieve these ends—what work there is to be done, and what types of people would be most qualified to do these tasks. In whatever capacity, these people should all be widowed. However, not everyone wants to provide service. Some may be more suited to do administrative work in a program, to develop social activities, to serve as officers and so forth.

The organizational structure for an outreach program need not be complex. There are people to reach out and people who need reaching. Thus, in the Widow-to-Widow program, the aides, armed with the names from death certificates, simply contacted those widows whose names they had. Record keeping is very important to keep track of who was reached, who accepted, and who refused. This is a job for a volunteer who may want to help but not reach out.

It is essential that volunteers come together for regular meetings to talk about what they are doing. At that time a review of records would reveal if anyone was missed. These meetings also provide opportunity to get moral support, and to learn from each other how to be more helpful.

Organizations change and grow, and must adjust to this. As with Widow-to-Widow, the expanded and changing program necessitated that the structure gradually change to accommodate the larger number of people involved, and the changing goals and needs. In setting up a program in the community, it is suggested that the structure have built-in flexibility to respond to acquired experience, enlarged goals, and increased numbers of participants. This is where the experience represented by the many groups at this workshop should be applied. For example, in a large social group for the widowed, an outreach service program or a hot line could be run by one committee of the organization.

How is the group to be perpetuated? The Widow-to-Widow program paid their employees to continue their work because it was located in a teaching center and had a research component. Once the idea has been demonstrated to be workable, this program should be absorbed by newly developing ones in the community. The success of the Widow-to-Widow program will be measured by its continuation, after leaving Harvard, to be run solely by and for the widowed primarily on a voluntary basis.

Other organizations need not feel the constraints the University's requirements put on the Widow-to-Widow program. But it still is necessary to have some regulations. If paying someone, how can it be determined that he has visited the bereaved? If depending on volunteers, what safeguards are there to insure that the job is done? First: make it mandatory that every volunteer attend the group meetings. Second: get good volunteers. Screening of volunteers achieves this. The Widow-to-Widow program discovered that there is a self-eliminating process at work. Because of the emotional content of the work, the person who tries this work and sticks to it, is usually well suited. However, some initial interviews may be in order to ensure that the volunteers are aware of what is involved in offering a service to others, are willing to share their personal experiences and have the capacity to listen.

In addition to goals, organization, structure, and staff, a most important aspect of this work is legitimation and funding. Consider funding first. The funds required will depend on how ambitious the program is. A program in a local community of about 30,000 (with about 6 people widowed in a month) could be run by widowed people in their spare time, thus requiring very minimal financial support. When asking for funds, it is always easier to raise money if possible contributors can see that the program is not just an idle dream but a small working reality. However, it might be useful to begin plans as if no money were available.

There are many models to follow for covering operating expenses. To maintain independence, Alcoholics Anonymous will accept no more than $100 in gifts from any one person in any one year. People from Parents Without Partners support themselves through dues collected from members. Betty Wilson has remarked, "If the widowed wait for someone to give them what they need or to recognize their plight, and then develop a program for them, defeat is just around the corner." The challenge for the widowed is to harness all the talent available and do the job with that.

Legitimation is still a different issue. Working in the community requires some permission. This is not to say that it is necessary to wait until someone in authority nods approval. Parents without Partners receives legitimation from their constituents of single parents who see this group as serving a legitimate need in their community. However, their stationery lists a professional advisory board who advises and guides them in making the special experience of the expert available to the members. The advisors are available in meeting unusual difficulties. Having clergymen, mental health professionals, physicians, even funeral directors sponsoring activities contributes to respectability—and lends authority when entering peoples' lives as in an outreach program for the newly widowed. It implies connection, and responsiveness to working with others. It is not necessary to take orders from these advisors; it is simply that they are available upon request in times of need. They will work with and for those involved in the program. They are allies who can help reach the widowed the program intends to serve. They may be salesmen to the non-widowed community as well, when that need arises.

In the Widow-to-Widow program I recruited local clergy and a settlement house who were interested in the needs of the widowed. It was fitting and proper for them to sponsor such activities in their community. Without their permission, Harvard Medical School had no business working in that community. They provided guidance . . . it was these agencies that suggested sending widows to widowers might not be a practical action. It was these agencies that interviewed the aides and established the salary scale. In starting new programs, most people will be members of the community they intend to serve, and therefore may not need the same legitimation as the Widow-to-Widow did. It would be expected that they know their community. However, to grow and progress, one needs allies and access to various experts who can help in a pinch. To some extent, the experience of the Widow-to-Widow program provides a type of legitimation, and by referring to this work and building from it, the task is easier.

Who sponsors the program, who makes up an advisory board, depends on the community and what people are available. However, it is necessary to stress the point that this is an advisory board and does not dictate policy, for it is the widowed who know best how to help other widowed individuals.

The issues, then, to be concerned with in establishing a program for an individual community are:

1. Goals

2. Organizational structure

3. Recruiting volunteers

4. Obtaining financial support

5. Receiving legitimation and additional expertise when needed.

These ideas can be checked against the experience reported next in Chapter VII as various individuals report on the development of their group for the widowed.

Chapter VII

ORGANIZATIONS FOR THE WIDOWED—
REPORTS FROM THE PARTICIPANTS

Included in this chapter are brief descriptions of various groups sponsored in the main by religious bodies, which operate by and for the widowed population and serve to meet the social and emotional needs of the people who join them.

Many of these groups have faced similar problems regardless of the fact that they often serve very different populations. One such difficulty arises when members remarry and wish to remain within the organization. There was general agreement by the representatives of the organizations that this is not always appropriate and can be self-defeating. Some groups have formed alumni associations, others simply state that remarriage constitutes the termination of their membership within the organization, after the current dues period.

Another common problem is the need to meet the demands of the various age groups that might be attracted to an organization. In a group which requires members to have dependent children, for example, there is a self-selection process. Depending on the conception and idea of the group, some organizations only attract older people while others attract those under 40. In many instances, needs are universal and age is irrelevant.

The problem of age becomes particularly critical in relation to people who still have families to raise and may wish to talk about their family problems and dating concerns. Most of the organizations represented agreed that the need to socialize is not a function of age but is a state of mind, and that this should be recognized. There should consequently be encouragement by organizational leadership to develop social programs for younger as well as older widowed people in the organizations. Separate committees devoted to the needs of different groups is one possible way to carry this suggestion through.

The following talks do not necessarily reflect the entire story of the origin of the groups. It may appear, while reading them, that the clergy were the initiators and instigators of the groups in response to a felt need. On the contrary, however, almost without exception, each of the groups started because one of several widowed people in the congregation or parish felt the need, and insisted, nagged, and generally pestered the organized religious body until it responded with the offer of sponsorship and assistance in forming such a group. The widowed had insisted that this was a service they wanted from the clergy, particularly as it was the clergy who could provide the most legitimate sponsorship.

None of the groups, to date, has done much systematic reaching-out to newly widowed people. If any occurs, it is strictly informal. Most of the organizations recruit members by advertising in local newspapers, parish or church bulletins and similar media. In this way, they depend upon the initiative of the widowed to seek out the organization. This may, indeed, leave a population of widowed whose needs are not met; but it does serve large numbers of people as testified by the many and various widowed groups represented.

Parents Without Partners has chapters throughout the country to which widows and widowers with dependent children would be attracted. As a result, large numbers of the widowed people present at these meetings are members of this organization. Since this organization's membership is primarily divorced people, the widowed in Parents Without Partners face different problems from those in groups for the widowed only. The participants saw this workshop as an opportunity to get ideas and perspective to help them provide more adequately for the special needs of the widowed in the context of Parents Without Partners.

Many people have spoken of how their respective groups had made it possible for them to recover from the crisis of widowhood. One young woman explained the meaning that Parents Without Partners held for her. Similar stories can be heard from members of other groups as well. This woman was twenty-eight years old when her husband died. She was told about Parents Without Partners by the family physician, but she didn't want to go. When she finally arrived there, she found she was the youngest in the chapter by about 10 years. However, she stayed long enough to discover she had much in common with the other members regardless of the age differences, and that she was experiencing the same problems as they. She discovered that a widow has to reach rock bottom to be able to begin again:

> Since then I have become a different person. I have worked with unwed mothers, helped in church preparing for weddings, and done many other things that I was never involved in before. Parents Without Partners was like a shot in the arm; it is people who have gone through common experiences. We have to be humble with those who come to us, and let them know

what we have been through. Then we can help them become whole persons and better parents.

A universal problem that plagues all the groups was lack of funds to expand or sometimes even to maintain ongoing programs. Since there is no simple solution to this problem, the focus of the brief descriptions of the groups centers on what available manpower and resources can accomplish.

Women's Fellowship Group
Church of the Ascension
Rochester, New York

The young Assistant Minister of our Church asked for a meeting with one of the widows to see how she felt about starting a Widows' Group. She agreed to form a committee to look into it. Seven widows met with the Minister and, as they talked, they became enthusiastic about the idea.

This committee had several more meetings and decided they would be a Steering Committe for one year. They composed a letter of invitation and mailed a copy to every known widow and single woman in the parish. You may question "single woman." However, the Committee, after much discussion, felt we should not be a closed group, but should include all women who are alone and wish to join.

As it worked out so far, our group consists of older women over fifty-five, with two single women, one divorcee, and the rest widows. The most interested members are in their late sixties and seventies. It has made us realize the need of these older women; they have been very lonely.

One woman told us that she never knew many people at Church, but now she has many friends. She is most unhappy if she has to miss one of our meetings or outings because of illness. When a member is ill, many others visit her, send cards, and keep in touch.

The original name of the group was "Women Alone Group," but so many people in the church objected to that title, we voted to change it to the "Women's Fellowship Group."

This group was formed for recreational purposes, because we have found that many of these women felt it had been years since they had had any "fun" in their lives. We have a dinner meeting every month, handled by a different committee each time. Each committee seems to have a good time getting together to plan for that month's activity. They get in touch with all members and arrange rides for those who do not drive. They make all arrangements for food if we are to eat at Church or, if we are going to a restaurant, they pick the place and make the reservations.

We meet ten months out of the year. Rochester winters are usually the most severe in January and February, so we run our meetings from March through December.

We have gone on short trips, picnics, had guests at our meetings to show travel slides, and many other activities.

Our second year is beginning with a new Steering Committee and many new outings are planned.

From the very start, we made up our minds not to be over-organized. It is a very relaxed and happy group, with the membership still growing. At present, we have thirty-one members and our usual attendance is between twenty to twenty-five at each monthly meeting. It has become a close-knit group which welcomes new members with great kindness. There are no cliques and, so far, it has been a group of women who show great concern for one another.

Mrs. Mary Butterfield
Mrs. Edith Kleisley

Catholic Widow and Widower Club
Hamilton, Ohio

The first meeting of a group of Catholic widows and widowers from the Hamilton area was held on April 3, 1970, in Hamilton, Ohio.

Father Richard Donovan, spiritual advisor, spoke of the need for an organization where those who share a common bond (the loss of a spouse by death) could unite and provide spiritual as well as cultural and social betterment of the members.

We organized immediately.

We have not been idle. Looking over the activities of the club for its first year, one cannot help but wonder what the second year will bring.

1970

Apr.   3: Organizational meeting.
May   1: Nomination and election of officers.
May   22: Installation Dinner.
June   5: Regular meeting. Dancing instructions.
June 28: Family picnic.
July 10: Regular meeting. Speaker on Social Security.
Aug.   7: Regular meeting. Speaker: Pastor—St. Peter's Church.

Aug. 19: Bus trip. Cincinnati Reds ball game.

Sept. 1: Regular meeting.

Sept. 6: Bus trip. Dayton, Ohio. Stage Play: "Mamo."

Sept. 13: Father Donovan died (heart attack).

Sept. 19: First marriage between members.

Sept. 28: Family picnic.

Oct. 2: Regular meeting. Film on highway safety.

Oct. 24: Halloween dance. St. Stephen's parish.

Nov. 1: Fun bowling party.

Nov. 6: Regular meeting. Dancing instructions.

Dec. 4: Regular meeting. Grapho-analyst demonstration. Donation given to Sisters of Poor for Christmas.

Dec. 15: Christmas party and dinner. Fun gift exchange.

Jan. 8: Regular meeting. Speaker—Bell Telephone Co.

Feb. 5: Regular meeting. Speaker and slides on A.I.D. service.

Feb. 14: Bus trip to Cincinnati. Ice Show (and the second marriage between members).

April 5: Regular meeting.

April 17: Dance—St. Ann's Hall.

Yes, it has been an active, busy year. Some members prefer to be in an "on the go" group, others in a "sitting" group; we try to please everyone.

After the meeting, those who wish can play cards, dance, play pool, and join in sing-a-longs, too. Life begins at forty? Well, it is also not too late for the fifties, sixties and seventies.

MARY H. BELL
President

Widows and Widowers Associated
Bridgeport, Connecticut

The first general meeting of Widows and Widowers Associated was held in February, 1969, in the Carlson Library of the University of Bridgeport under the sponsorship of the Council of Churches of Greater Bridgeport. It had been carefully planned through a series of small meetings and conferences.

There were approximately 125 present at that first meeting. Two years later we have a membership of well over 300 widows and widowers.

Meetings have been held consistently on the fourth Sunday evening of each month. Initially, they were held in various area church halls or the University of Bridgeport or Fairfield University, but recently, we were offered a permanent meeting place in St. George's Episcopal Church in Bridgeport.

In addition to our general meetings, we have planned and organized many group activities geared to the needs and interests of our members who range in age from the twenties through the seventies. Our average widowed person is employed, fairly young, and interested in active participation in the organization.

A brief resume of our group activities:

Service to the Widowed. A group which concerns itself with members who are ill or bereaved, or have other problems. They notify members, encourage visits to the hospitals, homes, or funeral homes, send cards, etc.

Discussion Groups. There are five separate discussion groups which meet monthly in the homes of the members, usually on Saturday evenings. Under the leadership of the chairman or moderator, topics of interest to the particular group are selected in advance, and discussed. A portion of the evening is purely social. At Christmas time, all groups united for a Christmas dinner and party.

Bowling. Our bowlers meet every Monday evening. They are a large group, well organized into teams. They marked the close of last season with an awards dinner.

Home Maintenance. This is a group which meets monthly in members' homes. Problems of home maintenance are presented and discussed. The members share their knowledge and skills.

Dancing. A group meets one evening a month in St. Paul's Episcopal Church hall.

Parents of Minor Children. These young parents have had many activities involving their children as well as social functions for themselves.

Knitting and Sewing. A group that meets in members' homes to enjoy fellowship while doing hand work.

Card Playing. Bridge groups and Pinochle groups.

Performing Arts. A group that is interested in music, dramatics, etc.

Hiking. A group that plans outdoor trips.

In addition, we have Open House every Saturday and Sunday evening at St. Paul's Episcopal Church. These meetings have been named "Do Nothings." All widowed people are welcome and there is no charge. Activities consist of card-playing, Bingo, checkers, line-dancing, what have you. They are very informal. Usually coffee and cake are served, but there also have been spaghetti suppers, pizza or hot dogs. These evenings are self-supporting. A basket is passed, and the returns have always more than covered the cost of refreshments. Many new members have joined us after dropping in at one of these evenings.

In addition, we have had many social functions—several theater parties, dinners, picnics, pot-luck suppers, and a trip to the Pennsylvania Dutch country.

The basic purpose of the organization is to promote programs that will enrich the lives of the widowed, and, through fellowship and shared experiences, help the bereaved and their families make a sound adjustment to an altered way of life.

In two years, we have achieved significant success in attaining these goals. Now we have been made increasingly aware of the great need for more organizations such as ours. Many of our members have been traveling considerable distances to join in our program and we have had a number of inquiries from widowed persons in widely-scattered areas. Some have been interested enough to visit us and have expressed the hope that eventually the widowed in their community would organize. As a result, we have felt impelled to share our experience by planning an expansion program. We realized that we could provide the catalyst that was lacking for these many widowed people.

A committee was formed to carry on this work. Its members are dedicated and experienced. Their first project was to organize the Widows and Widowers of Southern Fairfield County. Sponsored by the Stamford-Darien Council of Churches, this group has grown rapidly in a few short months.

The services of the committee are available to anyone interested in forming a local group.

CATHERINE STZURMA

DISCUSSION NOTES

The first question asked was how this group reached the newly bereaved. The group has a general monthly meeting which is advertised in the newspaper, which about 200 people attend. They prefer to work by referral with the newly bereaved to avoid intruding. Initially these people are invited to small discussion groups of about 10 or 12 people by personal letter, which may be followed up by a phone call. They are only invited to larger meetings when they are ready. People rarely ask where the group got their name, and if they initiate the call, the organization finds that they never learned about it from their clergy.

The issue of different age groups was discussed. Does an older group discourage the young from joining and do they have very different problems? Most groups do not make a distinction in age. There is a tendency for cliques to form, which although not always desirable, does happen. The parents of minor children do have a need to talk about their family problems, while the senior people feel they have raised their children and have a right to enjoy themselves. The groups felt that their association does tend to neglect the young widow with children. One solution was to try to get some of the older women to help with babysitting so the young widows can get out. They have a policy not to divide groups by ages. One reason is that it is difficult to know where to put the dividing line. Who is old? Some seventy-four year olds are young, and some young widows are already old.

They Help Each Other Spiritually (THEOS)
Pittsburgh, Pennsylvania

THEOS was founded February, 1962, in Pittsburgh, Pennsylvania, by Bea Decker. Mrs. Decker had recently lost her husband and realized the need for an organization where she and others could learn to live again and cope with the many problems which had to be faced. THEOS has been geared to the needs of the young and middle-aged widowed person specializing in the major transition period and assisting in the rebuilding of their lives, including helping the children involved.

There are presently three chapters of THEOS in Pittsburgh and one in the process of being established. Chapters also have been organized in Chambersburg, Pennsylvania, Baltimore, Maryland, Salem, Oregon, and Seattle, Washington. It is intended that more chapters will be formed in other parts of the United States.

A significant portion of the programs of the chapters consists of well-informed, inspirational, and educational speakers and panel discussions concerning subjects of interest to the widowed. The social activity of these groups is family-oriented and is limited to the rehabilitation and helping of the bereaved. The members of these groups are encouraged to assist each other and to engage in civic activities. THEOS works in conjunction with other organizations such as Alcoholics Anonymous and Big Brothers.

A monthly newsletter is published and mailed to approximately five hundred persons. This newsletter contains information regarding the activities and programs of the various chapters, publications offered by THEOS, spiritual quotations, references to literature in related fields, and general civic information. The civic information includes notices of programs of interest to widowed persons sponsored by YMCAs, local churches, information concerning counseling services, and information regarding needs of charitable organizations.

THEOS has conducted four successful weekend conferences at Kappel Lodge, a conference center near Pittsburgh. The conferences consist of small group seminars concerning various problems of widowhood with guest speakers who are experts in the field of widowhood. Participants, who had learned of THEOS through various kinds of publicity, have come from all areas of the United States. THEOS has received national and worldwide recognition; its work has been written up in eight national magazines and the founder has been interviewed on the Voice of America Radio Program as well as appearing on various television programs. Gladys Kooiman, key speaker at a Conference, was so impressed with the effect on lives, that she presently is co-authoring a book with the founder relating experiences since THEOS' conception. Mrs. Kooiman is author of *When Death Takes a Father*.

The newest venture is to conduct a series of group experiences for the widowed. This series is being done in conjunction with the Lutheran Service Society in Pittsburgh. The purpose of the series is to enable the widowed to work through their grief. The group will be led by clergy who have had specialized training in group experiences as well as the emotional implications of grief. The series will run for ten weeks and will deal with problems of family and personal life of the widowed. The agenda for discussions will be determined by the participants themselves. The group will be backed up by a team of psychiatrists, psychologists, and social workers who are available to handle the particular concerns of each individual.

THEOS is unique in that it has no by-laws, constitution, dues, or membership. A free will offering is received which is used to maintain the work of the local group or groups. The work can best be summed up in the words of a widow:

> I feel it has helped me because I needed someone who understood my problem. No one can describe the need for someone, only those who have been through this grief themselves.

No organization can end the heartaches of the bereaved, but sharing the burden with others helps to lighten it.

BEA DECKER
Founder

Post Cana
Washington, D.C.

Post Cana is an association of widowed people, both men and women, which was formed in the Metropolitan area of Washington, D.C., in 1960. Its purpose was to aid widows and widowers, and to assist and promote the solution of those spiritual, parental, psychological, financial, social and other problems arising directly or indirectly from the untimely death of a husband or wife. We have found that widowed people have a common bond which encourages a relaxed and symbiotic environment.

Post Cana is part of the Family Life Movement which is sponsored by the Archdiocese of Washington but membership in Post Cana is open to widowed persons of all denominations regardless of age, who never have been divorced.

Our programs are varied and intended to accommodate the interests and needs of all Post Cana members. We try to provide something for everyone.

To carry out these purposes, programs are instituted at two levels: the regionally divided groups and the central body. The local group has proven better suited for intensive exploration of the individual challenges and particular methods of rising to them such as, group therapy, discussion and mutual help.

The governing body of Post Cana is the executive council, comprised of the officers, committee chairman and group leaders under the guidance of its Moderator, the Archdiocesan Director of Family Life Bureau. The function of the executive council is to carry out the purposes and objectives of the movement at the Archdiocesan level, to establish and maintain an effective organization; to consider for approval, proposals and programs of various committees and local groups and to generally coordinate plans and operations in the interest of a strong, unified Post Cana organization.

The group leader is responsible for guiding activities of a group usually composed of from six to twenty members; for scheduling meetings, for contacting prospective members, and for maintaining contact with the clergy of the area from which group members are drawn.

The Priest (or other clerical) Moderator of each area provides practical guidance to the newly widowed, as well as spiritual comfort. He informs each widowed person about Post Cana by letter or in person, helps to organize Post Cana groups, schedules a meeting in the church hall, auditorium or library, provides counselling, leads discussions or appoints an assistant to act as counselor for the group, enlists the assistance of members of other organizations to serve on advisory committees, on legal, financial, educational and other practical matters.

Yearly programs on both levels are designed to provide balanced, spiritual, intellectual and social activities. By these means, members are assisted not only in meeting their own problems but, hopefully, also trained to help other widowed families.

A group recently organized calling itself "Counter Foil" to meet the needs of members of Post Cana under forty years of age.

Louise B. Duffy
Publicity Chairman

Parents Without Partners
44 Wood Avenue
East Longmeadow, Massachusetts

Parents Without Partners, Inc. is an international non-profit, non-sectarian, educational organization devoted to the welfare and interests of single parents and their children.

What Is A 'Single Parent'?

A single parent is a person who is the parent of one or more living sons or daughters and who is single by reason of death, divorce, separation, or never-married, or by other reasons which may be deemed acceptable by Parents Without Partners, International. Custody of children is not a factor of eligibility.

What's 'Educational' About Parents Without Partners?

Many and acute are the peculiar problems of bringing up children alone, or in contending with "visitation rights" and all the other adjustments, ambiguities and emotional conflicts arising out of post-widowedhood and post-separation. Parents Without Partners, Inc., is the only national and international organization that exists to study these problems, to provide a meeting-place for discussing them, and to develop programs for their solution. Through programs of discussions, professional speakers, study groups, newsletters, and international publications, real help is provided to the confused and isolated to find himself/herself and to reshape his/her own life to meet the unique and unpredictable conditions of single-parenthood.

Organizational Structure

The International Board of Directors includes Zone Staff (six zones in United States and one zone in Canada) composed of Zone Administrators, Associate Zone Administrators, and District Supervisors. There are Regional Councils and almost 500 Chapters chartered throughout the United States, Canada and Australia with a membership of over 60,000 single-parent families. Its programs and activities are entirely the volunteer work of members of Parents Without Partners, Inc.

Preamble to the Constitution of Parents Without Partners, Inc.

As conscientious single parents, it is our primary endeavor to bring our children to healthy maturity, with the full sense of being loved and accepted as persons, and with the same prospects for normal life as children who mature in a two-parent home.

From the divorce or separation which divides a family, or the loss of a parent by death, it is the child who suffers most. For children in such circumstances to grow unscarred requires the utmost in love, understanding, and sound guidance. To provide these is a responsibility inherent in parenthood. It does not end with separation or divorce, for either parent.

The single parent in our society is isolated to some degree. The difficulties of providing both for ourselves and our children a reasonable equivalent of normal family life, is increased by that isolation. The established pattern of community life lacks both means of communication and institutions to enable us to resolve our special problems, and find normal fulfillment.

Therefore, in the conviction that we can achieve this and through working together, through the exchange of ideas, and through the mutual understanding, help and companionship which we find with one another, we have established "PARENTS WITHOUT PARTNERS, INC." to further our common welfare and the well-being of our children.

AMIGOS Program.

The Amigos Program at Parents Without Partners, which greets and works with newly bereaved members for sixty days is operant in only one Chapter that we know of in Buffalo, New York. The Amigos accompany the new member to Parents Without Partners' functions. They will also accompany them to other places as well. This very important program should be extended to every

Chapter, since at first many people are afraid of strange large groups.

Patricia H. Devine
International Director
Springfield, Mass.

Naim Conference
Chicago, Illinois

Naim came into being in 1957. Its founders were Jean and Bill Delaney, who had the cooperation of the late Father Timothy Sullivan. Jean and Bill had both been widowed, and after their marriage to each other, thought of the many things that could be done on behalf of the widowed by those who had already experienced such a loss. With Father Sullivan they set out to see what could be done to establish an organization to assist the widowed.

In 1958 a Forum was planned for St. Patrick's Church in Chicago. The newspapers were quite generous with publicity and the planners were overwhelmed at the number who responded—over 800, in all. This told of the need of widowed people for someone to understand them and their special status in life.

Soon chapters were started, primarily on a geographical basis. Now we have twenty-seven chapters in the Chicago area and four in the Rockford diocese. Originally, each chapter was represented at headquarters by delegates, but, eventually, a Council was formed, and the president of each chapter meets at Naim headquarters once each month to plan programs, to discuss needs, to formulate spiritual programs, discussion meetings and family activities which are centered around the children and their parents. We had monthly discussion meetings during the first part of this year, which focused on spiritual and moral needs, and included a psychologist who spoke on growth and grief. Because many of our members have children about to enter college, we had one program geared to scholarships—their availability and requirements. This discussion was very well attended by members and their high school age children.

During Father Sullivan's tenure, indoctrination programs were held. Anyone interested in Naim was asked to attend three consecutive indoctrination programs, after which they could, if they desired, join a chapter.

We now have what we term conferences and, under Father Corcoran's guidance, these are held as frequently as we can schedule them. We try to rotate them around the city so that all sections are covered. At these conferences, we usually have a widow and a widower speak on the problems of adjustment, a lawyer who talks on financial and legal problems faced by widowed people, and Father Corcoran conducts a discussion period which takes in the spiritual aspects of widowhood. These programs are from 2:00 to 5:00 P.M. on Sunday afternoons. We feel they are the best introduction to Naim and strongly urge widowed people to attend a conference before going to a chapter. Most people agree that this is the most effective way of being introduced to Naim. We had fifteen conferences last year and, so far this year, have had nine, with several more in the planning stage. We learn of those who need our services in many ways. Often, an interested friend or relative contacts Naim and suggests that we send information on Naim to the widowed person. Many priests send us names of their parishioners who become widowed. Sometimes newspapers who receive inquiries about organizations relative to the widowed send these inquiries on to us.

We are at present hoping to enlarge our panelist group. We are very well pleased with our present speakers; they do an excellent and dedicated job—but they are not indestructible, so we don't want them to wear themselves out.

Socially, we have at least four all-chapter socials during each year which attracted the entire membership. Most of the chapters have dances, card parties, dinner affairs, to which they invite the other chapters. Among our family activities are picnics (at least three each summer), bowling, skating, costume parties at Halloween, and a grand Christmas party for all the youngsters, which, for the last three years, has been held at Holy Name Cathedral. This party includes a tableau about the Holy Family, gifts individually chosen and presented by Santa Claus, good things to eat and drink, candies to take home, and a completely happy time for all the youngsters, and a tiring but enjoyable time for the parents who participate in the work.

Whenever something is proposed that we haven't as yet tried, Father Corcoran gets a committee together, and we evaluate this new idea. He feels nothing should be overlooked if it could conceivably make life a little happier or fuller for our widowed people.

Orville Plummer

DISCUSSION NOTES:

Naim is a sectarian organization and a question was raised about how non-Catholics can relate to the group. While they are not accepted as members, they can attend social functions. Some non-Catholics were stimulated by their contact with Naim to form groups in their own church.

The problem of people who remarried and how they relate to the group was raised. It was pointed out that for the most part they leave the group. Sometimes they have formed a kind of alumni group. Some chapters do allow them to remain as members, most don't. There is a general rule in Naim that if they are holding office when they remarry they are allowed to complete their term of office up to one year after the wedding.

Usually people who remarry maintain a special relationship with the group. They often want to return some of what they have received. An example was cited of a lawyer who remarried and now is very helpful on the conference panels for the newly widowed. People who remarry don't need the group anymore; they stay to make a contribution. It was felt that for a newly widowed person to join Naim and find married people there would be very confusing. People who develop close friends in the group can go on seeing them socially. It is unhealthy to cling to Naim when they are starting a new life.

Eschaton Club
100 Arch St.
Boston, Massachusetts

The Eschaton Club is an organization for widowed people which meets weekly in the auditorium at St. Anthony's Shrine on Arch Street in Boston. It was started in late 1969, by a small group of widowed people. The good Fathers at the Shrine were approached and were happy to sponsor such a group. Week by week, the club grew, proving the need for a weekly social evening for the widowed.

The club has only one requirement for membership, and that is being widowed. We have members from several faiths who understand that while we meet in the auditorium of a Catholic Church, with a priest as moderator, the club is non-sectarian.

We try to provide a varied program to please everyone. This includes dancing lessons, movies, singing groups, lectures on drugs, handwriting, astrology, several dinners and dances, and trips. Square dancing is a big success each time we have it. We have bingo and nights for card playing and just socializing. We have had family nights, too.

We usually have from sixty-five to one hundred people there each week. We provide coffee and snacks brought in by the members themselves. I have met many fine people there and enjoy these new friends.

I realize that we don't satisfy everyone, but we try. I do know we have helped many people, and this is the main function of our organization.

Arthur Churchill
President

Carmel Club
North Shore Shopping Center
Peabody, Mass.

The Carmel Club is a social organization for widowed people founded in 1967 by Father Mark Dittami. Father Mark brought a special expertise to his role as founder; along with the guidance and counselling he could give as a clergyman, he could also understand what it was like to be widowed. Before becoming a priest, he had been a married man. After the death of his wife, he joined the Carmelite Order and it was while he was stationed at the Carmelite Chapel in Peabody, Massachusetts, that he was asked to form a group for widowed people.

Meetings are held twice a month—one a business meeting and the other social. Elected officers, together with committee members, plan and direct the various functions of the group. Membership now totals 135 widowed people, and since they have outgrown their quarters in Peabody, meetings are held in a very pleasant V.F.W. hall in Beverly.

Father Mark recently was transferred and another priest has taken his place as moderator.

John Conlon
President

Chapter VIII

NOTES FROM THE CONFERENCE
FOR WIDOWED ONLY

By Ruby Abrahams and Cécile Strugnell

The purpose of these small discussion groups was to give the participants a chance to detail how they would develop a program for the widowed in their own communities, using as a basis the steps outlined by Phyllis Silverman.

The first meeting, planned in advance by the staff, was devoted to letting the participants share more personally their experiences as widows and widowers and their expectations of the weekend. The focus for the evening meeting emerged from this preliminary discussion.

As it turned out, in the five workshops, much the same material was covered. It is, therefore, possible to present this composite of what took place. In essence, these meetings dealt with the feelings of the participants about programming for the widowed, and looked at the problems they would encounter in carrying out any plan they might conceive, with some attempt being made to find solutions for these difficulties.

First Meeting

Some of the people came to the weekend, hoping that it would provide them with an opportunity to discuss their personal needs. It was quickly apparent to all that, except insofar as such discussion could help them understand the needs of other widowed people, the workshop was not going to directly help them learn to cope better as widows. This conflict of interest was raised very early in these small meetings.

Meeting so many other widowed people changed some people's orientation. Some discovered, "It could be exciting to think of starting a program rather than just talk of widowhood." Others were aware that by trying to meet the needs of others, they fulfilled their own needs. One woman put it most succinctly,

> I wanted something for myself; that's why I joined an organization. It never occurred to me to give anything. This workshop has made me realize the need to give.

Most of the issues raised were related to programming needs:

1. How to start a group for the widowed, distinguishing between a large metropolitan community and a smaller town.

    a. How best to help the newly widowed in a one-to-one outreach, while respecting their privacy.

    b. How to recruit, select and train people to reach out.

    c. How to find the newly widowed.

2. How to start a telephone line.

3. Existing groups wanted to know how to focus less on social activities and become more service-oriented, with particular emphasis on how to better meet the needs of the newly widowed, the young widow or widower with children, and others with special needs.

For members of chapters of Parents Without Partners, this was especially true, since much of their programming succeeds best with divorced single parents.

4. How to reach and involve more widowers.

5. How to get the cooperation and understanding of the professionals, including the clergy.

6. How to finance a program.

7. How to handle internal dissensions and organizational problems of any group that will be formed or is now in existence.

Second Meeting

1. *Types of Outreach*

Meeting the special needs of the newly widowed was the strongest concern in all the groups. Having realized that the newly bereaved are often not ready to come out and join a group, but need someone to reach out to them, how can their needs be met?

The Widow-to-Widow Program and several existing widowed groups have experimented in three types of outreach:

a. The one-to-one outreach, leading to an ongoing personal relationship, if needed.

One young Parents Without Partners widow picked this as the most meaningful thing which can be done for the new widow:

I had attended discussion meetings myself and they had left me cold. Later a friend of mine became widowed and was in very bad shape. Wanting to help her, I invited her to come to Parents Without Partners discussions. I don't think I really helped her much. Now I know what I should have done. I should have invited her into my own kitchen, sat down with her over a cup of coffee, listened to her, allowed her to talk and express her feelings to me. For me, the one-to-one relationship is the really meaningful help for someone newly bereaved. Besides, some people just are not group-oriented and, for them, the one-to-one is the only help. I am going home now, determined to do some outreaching of my own.

b. Offering special programs for the newly widowed.

Some of the existing organizations have recognized that the new widow is not ready to join the group as a whole, mixing with people at different stages of bereavement. They need to be helped through certain problems specific to their stage of bereavement. These special programs can be an effective means of reaching a large number of people still recently widowed and in need of help to adjust to their new status. These programs, however, still will leave out those who are not ready to take the initiative to come out, and those who are not sufficiently group-oriented or in good enough shape to look for this kind of help.

c. Giving support to bring someone into the group.

In some organizations, there has been some personal outreach to newly bereaved people in the community, with the intention of helping them by bringing them into the widowed group. In this case, the initiative is not left to the newly widowed, and there is some one-to-one contact involved, though it only develops if the newly bereaved is interested in the help that can be provided through the group.

2. *How to Find the Newly Widowed*

a. *Death Certificates.* These are public documents. There was some reluctance to use this method. It was considered as an intrusion on people's privacy by some. None of the newly widowed participants in the Widow-to-Widow program expressed any concern about this to any of the aides.

b. *Obituaries:* Considered especially effective in a smaller community where the local newspaper will provide total coverage for that particular community.

c. *Referrals From Professionals:* This led to a discussion of the reluctance of the various professionals to get involved and recognize the needs of the widowed. The clergy would seem an obvious resource, especially as the parish or congregation structure provides coverage of a limited geographic area. The clergy have not been generally willing to make such referrals or even to provide names of newly widowed people. They often are not even willing to inform the newly widowed of existing groups in their community. Even trying to work with them over a period of years, sending them notices several times a year, has produced very little result. More often, it is friends of the bereaved who are likely to refer them.

Parents Without Partners has put a great deal of effort in getting their work known in the community. They see referrals from professionals who are in touch with the newly bereaved as the only way of reaching people in a large city. They have sent their literature to lawyers, doctors, clergy, mental health workers. Gradually, these professionals have cooperated.

Some thought the reluctance to refer newly widowed people was based on a certain suspicion as to what we can do for them, as well as a reluctance on the part of the professionals to admit that they cannot help.

Funeral directors also were considered as a possible source of names. There was some hesitancy in working closely with them in large cities where this service is provided by large, impersonal corporations.

d. *Publicity Through Newspaper Articles, or on Radio or T.V.:* All are ways of reaching the newly bereaved, but still this requires their taking the initiative to call in or come to meetings. One way of starting a publicity campaign would be to send out a press release to the participants' local newspaper mentioning the workshop and giving them names so that widowed people may contact them. A series of articles on the problems of the widowed might also focus attention on the issues and needs of this program.

e. *Other Special Sources of Names:* Some widows present had personal contacts or worked with Welfare or a mental health agency. Another suggested getting names from the Public School Guidance Department. One widower was personnel manager of his company and therefore had access to newly widowed personnel in his company.

The methods used would differ depending on the size of the community involved. The larger community would have to be split up geographically; several church congregations or settlement houses could provide areas of a size in which it would be practical to work.

3. *Methods of Contacting the Widowed*

Several methods have been used in first contacts with the newly bereaved:

a. A series of letters:

—a condolence note, introducing the sender and organization;

—six to eight weeks later—a letter asking if they need any help;

—three to four months later—a phone call. Ask again if they need any help and try to arrange to visit with him/her.

b. Send a letter making an appointment about three weeks after the death, giving phone number in case the appointment is not convenient.

c. Send a note, inviting the newly bereaved to come out to a small discussion meeting. Follow up on this with a phone call, making a one-to-one contact, and offering to pick them up to go to the meeting.

There was a great deal of discussion as to the time when a widow is ready to be approached. There seems to be a great deal of variation according to individual cases:

To me, the hardest time was about a year after his death.

One participant had been served by the Widow-to-Widow Program:

When I got the letter, I put it away and thought that was not for me. It was about five months later, one day when I felt down, that I got the letter out and called Mary. . . .

Generally speaking, three weeks after seemed the earliest time possible, preference being given to waiting a longer period.

d. In instances where someone is referred to an organization, a phone call is made or a letter is usually sent promptly thereafter. Some one-to-one exchange takes place then, but, mostly, the emphasis is on helping the widowed to come to meetings.

4. *Who Can Do the Outreach?*

Characteristics required for the widow or widower helper:

He or she must have recovered from his/her grief;

—needs to be able to talk about it;

—needs to have listening skills;

—needs to have "guts" to go out and make the first visit on own initiative;

—must be secure enough that he or she does not feel rejected, if the bereaved says "no", or refuses to open the door;

—needs to have a commitment to helping others.

Listening skills involve the capacity to tune in to the problems and real needs of the widowed person, who may not always be able to express those needs, or accept them as a normal part of being widowed. For example, the person who asks about clubs and social activities, really may be saying that she finds it difficult to go out and be among people. She may need to be put in contact with one person, who will take her and introduce her to the club, or she may need just to talk about her loneliness for a while. The caller to the Service Line, who says she called to find out what the program is about, is usually hedging on what the real problem is and it may take time and more than one call to get through to her.

Group meetings of volunteers are very helpful in developing listening skills and self-confidence. These should be held at least once a month. Experiences of helping are shared and discussed. The volunteers may pool their own experiences as widows and widowers and mutually help each other to understand the helping process and the needs of the widowed. The support mutually given by these meetings is essential to volunteers engaged in this work.

Volunteers are helped themselves in the process by helping and, after a certain time in the volunteer group, they may become ready to move on to other activities in the community. This should be encouraged.

> Our volunteers are an everchanging group. There is a nucleus of people who have been around for a while and who stay with the organization . . . but for most of them, once they begin to adjust and when they are ready to go out into the community and get involved in other things—they do, and they leave our organization, which is fine . . . This is our purpose.

5. *What Is Helping?*

Someone asked: "Just what do you say to another widow that is different?"

The following points emerge from the discussions:

It is not what you say; it is the fact that another widow can *listen*, unlike friends and family, who have been saying, "Keep a stiff upper lip." There is value in the fact that she is a stranger. She does not own you; she cannot take over or smother you; she did not know your husband, but she can share the common experience of grief. She provides the opportunity for sharing and support, *not* dependency.

What are the feelings the newly widowed may have?

In some cases, she may have guilt feelings about something she did or did not do in connection with her husband's death, but this is rare. More often, she may have feelings of remorse or regret; she may wish she had done things differently, or handled this or that in another way, though there is no feeling of self-blame. The helper should distinguish between these two states of feeling: guilt or remorse.

It is important to remember that the newly bereaved does not feel like a widow. Other people see her as that. Until she accepts her role, she is in a suspended state. A woman with small children tends to know sooner that she is a widow. Her needs are immediate and she accepts help sooner; the older woman can hide for much longer. In learning to be a widow, she has to look at the past, not live in the past. Living in the past, she sees herself as her husband's wife, still living in his shadow, acting in a way that would have pleased him. The emphasis still is on her husband and his wishes, and not on herself as a widow. She needs to believe she can change or grow, and not be bound to the past. She needs to learn that she can do things by and for herself. Another widow, who has grown and adjusted to the single role, presents an example ("If

116

she can do it, so can I"). The adjusted widow can share her experience of how she went about accepting that role. The widow or widower who is helping also has to believe that people can learn and grow.

What is involved in listening? The following suggestions were made:

—Do not make positive statements.

—Talk about what you found good in your own situation and let the newly bereaved think about it.

—You are no different from the widow and widowers you are trying to reach and aid. Therefore, you have a special ability to emphathize and your own experience to draw on.

—In recalling your own experience, equip yourself with an outline of your helplessness at that time and what could have been done to alleviate the problems.

—Each person goes through his own individual way of mourning and of showing sorrow.

—Start only with those you think can help.

—The length of your visit depends on what transpires.

—Do not make a contact on a day you do not feel like doing it. Too much contacting of the newly widowed can be emotionally exhausting. Take a few days off, when necessary.

—You do not want to lose your amateur standing. You do not want to become professionals.

—The widow-to-widow aid works, if you keep it simple—just one widow or widower talking to another widow or widower.

Sometimes a person will not bring out his/her feelings on the first contact. The first interview, or telephone call, may involve only a neighborly chat, or giving information on very specific problems, such as legal, financial, or child-raising problems. Talking on these issues builds up confidence in the helper. It is then helpful to call back. The emotional problems or feelings may come out during the second or subsequent conversations. Sometimes the person is reluctant to receive a face-to-face visit, though the bereaved may be ready to talk openly on the telephone. Or, the converse may be true. The helper has to learn to listen and *hear* what the bereaved is asking for. At some point, every new widow needs the opportunity to get out her feelings. The helper can help her to cry, when she needs it. Moreover, the widow helper can go on listening, because she understands, when family and friends no longer want to hear about it. For some time, the bereaved may have a need to go on talking about her husband and his death. This is normal in the period of mourning, which can last for weeks, or months.

There is no need to feel guilty or apologetic about past bereavement behavior. The widow helper can give perspective to this. She may tell the bereaved, "Sure, you are going to act nutty, obnoxious at times, and be like everyone else in this boat."

Some of the participants expressed their feelings like this:

> . . . they may have to get their feelings out only once, or it may take longer . . . but you have to help them to get those feelings out . . .

> It may take as long as three years to realize that you really are a widow. Something snaps and all of

> a sudden you realize you no longer have a husband to care for . . .

> I feel that I have been thrust into a role I did not ask for . . . I am not less of a person, but I am disabled . . .

Eventually, the person who has been helped may go on to helping. Helping is a two-way process: the helper is helped.

> Helping others helped me. I learned about the problems of others. When people come to me, I can relate it to my own experience . . ."

> My salvation is to give. You forget yourself . . . in giving . . . hearing others, you learn to know yourself better . . .

Different needs at different stages of bereavement may have to be met by different types of programs. To cover these needs, a program may have to include:

a. Widow-to-widow outreach to the newly bereaved on a one-to-one basis.

b. The discussion group situation for those who are ready to share their feelings with a group. This seems to be particularly appropriate for the younger widowed, with young children to raise.

c. The social group. This may be more appropriate for the longer-term widowed, who still feel more comfortable in a group of widowed people, and who need the contacts for socializing.

d. Mechanisms for helping people to become more service-oriented. Any program should be flexible enough to allow the person helped to become a helper, and to move continuously into expanded responsibilities if he/she wishes to continue in the program.

6. *Procedures for Setting Up New Programs*

a. *Form a Group of Helpers:* Form a nucleus of interested people to help and work with you. The frustrations of developing and maintaining an organization are considerable. There is only so much that one person can do. The personal needs of the leaders of the group have to be taken into account. Each person has to find for himself a satisfactory balance between his own needs, the needs of his family, and the needs of the organization. You cannot spare people who get immersed in organization and neglect other things. You can only warn them of what may be ahead, pointing to ways of finding a balance. Very often, it falls to a small group of people to get the job done. This makes it easy for a potential group to become a one-man show. To avoid this, share and assign to others the jobs that need to be done.

b. *Community Sponsorship and Legitimation:* Find a sponsor, or group of sponsors in the community. Clergymen, lawyers, funeral directors, bank trust officers, local chambers of commerce, community service organizations—like the YWCA or Council of Churches—may be approached. Such sponsorship gives the program legitimation in the community. When you contact the widowed, with this sponsorship behind you, they are less likely to think you are just prying or to misinterpret your intentions. It is important to have the support of the local community. Sometimes, it is necessary to make a pest of yourself to get this support. It may be essential to reach only the members of the same sex to avoid any misunderstanding of intentions.

c. *Public Relations and Educating the Community:* Publicize the program in newspapers, T.V., radio, church bulletins and in any way which will help to educate the community to the needs of the widowed and the services you can provide. Clarify your aims so that when you contact the newly widowed, your intentions will be known. See to it initially that widows see widows and widowers widowers until the program is established and above suspicion. Written material on bereavement and the Widow-to-Widow Program is available. (See Bibliography).

d. *Educating Professionals and Forming an Advisory Board:* You may form an Advisory Board of interested professionals, such as clergy, funeral directors, lawyers, physicians, mental health workers. Our experience at the workshop indicated that most of the widowed organizations around the country had received poor cooperation from professionals in the community, including clergy.

The task of educating the professionals to the needs of the widowed is a heavy one and hardly begun. Many professionals are hostile to the notion that non-professionals can be effective caregivers, and the idea that the widowed are best helped by other widows and widowers has little acceptance in professional circles. Yet, these professionals should be a good source of referral for the widowed in need of help. A major task before us all is to educate the professionals in the community to understand the needs of widowed people and the kind of help that is given by other widows and widowers in a mutual aid program.

The members of the Advisory Board also may offer consultation on specific problems, such as legal or financial matters.

e. *Listing of Community Resources:* In order to be more helpful to the bereaved, and to increase the self-confidence of the volunteer helper, a listing of community resources should be made available to him. This listing may include financial information about benefits for the widowed and where to go for financial advice, legal information, job training and employment facilities, where to go for full/part-time or work-at-home employment, listing of all available volunteer activities, health clinics, family clinics and services, social clubs for the widowed and singles clubs in the area. Facilities for the elderly and any special services which might be useful, such as a Suicide Line, Alcoholics Anonymous and similar organizations also should be included. It takes time to gather this information for any one community and it should be updated and added to at regular intervals. The Red-Feather-United Fund Agency could be helpful in getting this done.

A portfolio containing this information should be given to all new helpers.

f. *Funding:* A volunteer organization can be started with very little money. Some of the existing organizations began with some fund-raising activities, and then developed a membership, dues-paying system. Others have started and functioned on small donations from community sources, or voluntary donations at lectures, talks and discussion group sessions.

g. *Group Meetings For the Caregivers:* Once a group of helpers has been formed, there is a need for them to meet on a regular basis to discuss and share their experiences in trying to help the bereaved. These meetings serve several purposes:

(1) Mutual education and consultation among those widowed who are doing the helping.

(2) Giving each other mutual support and confidence in their work so they do not feel isolated in their difficulties; giving them a sense of community in their work.

(3) Giving them a chance to talk about their experiences in helping is necessary if this kind of work is not to get them down. This sharing gives them perspective and an opportunity to work through their own feelings.

This group also might be the place where a professional could act as consultant, helping the non-professionals to view their work with perspective and giving them extra support and back-up. This also would provide them with an opportunity to bring up unusual problems and discuss possible referrals to agencies in the community.

7. *Needs of Some Special Groups*

a. *The Younger Widow or Widower, with Young Children:* The young widowed, with small children, are the most likely to seek help in the early stages of their bereavement. This was found both in the Widow-to-Widow Program and on the Widowed Service Line. The needs of this group are immediate and pressing. There are often financial and child care problems, as well as the tasks of readjustment. Outreach to these younger people, in the first few weeks of the bereavement, often is helpful and welcomed. The discussion group situation also is welcomed fairly soon by this group. They can benefit by sharing their experience in adjusting to the single role, the single parent role, the handling of dating and sex problems. In Parents Without Partners, some of these group discussions are led by psychologists, or other mental health professionals. Such discussion sessions also can be led by a perceptive widow or widower, who has adjusted to the single role and the single parent role. These discussion groups probably are most effective when limited to a small number (not more than six to eight persons).

b. *The Children of the Widowed:* Children have their own problems of adjustment to the loss of a parent. It was suggested that, sometimes, they need to talk to someone outside the family—the parish priest was found to be helpful in one instance.

Some of the organizations represented have set up family programs, in which there are activities for the children, for teenagers, and for the whole family. The Big Brother organization is helpful for boys and it was suggested that many colleges have programs in which students are helpful to youngsters, especially teenagers.

c. *The Widower:* The special problems of the widower were given their due emphasis at this workshop. His major problem is housekeeping and child care, where there are young children. There were a legion of stories about unsatisfactory housekeepers. Many of the younger widowers seem to feel threatened by the housekeeper, who is more interested in him than in his children. It was suggested that widows with grown families, who like children and have the time, might offer their services in motherless homes.

The widower also may have financial problems. He does not receive Social Security payments, unless he has minor children and can collect on his wife's earnings under covered employment, and expenses of housekeeping and child care are heavy. His income, which was adequate when his wife was alive, is no longer adequate for these extra expenses. There seems to be few services in the community to help the widower in the care of his home and children.

Thirdly, the problem of loneliness and isolation is as acute for the widower as it is for the widow. One widower told of how much relief he had found in being able to talk to some other widowers at work and to find that his reactions to his problem were normal and felt by others. They shared their experiences of how these problems were handled.

Another widower told of his isolation because his in-laws blamed him for his wife's death. Then his children would have nothing to do with the in-laws. He described situations where a man is quite lost; for example, buying the daughter's first bra and how to discuss dating relationships with the adolescent girl.

Several widowers talked of their feelings of vulnerability. In their loneliness and need, they are afraid of being rejected, and are not comfortable in the company of other women. This makes the widowers reluctant to join groups where they always are outnumbered by widows. They have not been dating for years. They do not know how to act.

Finally, the widower may have conflicts concerning sex, morality and loyalty feelings:

. . . it feels like there is someone looking over your shoulder every minute . . .

. . . I don't feel comfortable around other women . . .

After these discussions, there were comments from some of the widows that they never had realized before what problems the men had in learning to approach women again. They felt they could be more understanding and helpful in the future, and less resentful when the men at a dance stayed congregated around the bar.

Loneliness, Dating, Sex

Both widows and widowers voiced their concern about their difficulties in relating again to members of the opposite sex. Some Parents Without Partners members felt that it is most helpful for men and women to meet each other around group activities that do not require pairing off, such as classes, sports and card games.

Some of the widowers said they were better helped by widows than by widowers with some of their problems. A number of widowers who have called the Widowed Service Line have preferred to talk to a woman, and some of the widow callers have enjoyed talking to a man. This may depend on the nature of the caller's problem and also whether the volunteer feels comfortable talking to the opposite sex, when this is a first contact with a stranger on the telephone.

The role of the professional consultant in a mutual help program was only touched on briefly. The focus here was on what the widowed themselves could do. There were some questions about what to expect from such a person and how to work with him.

Chapter IX

THE ROLE OF THE PROFESSIONAL IN A MUTUAL HELP ORGANIZATION

Some Informal Ideas on This Subject

By Phyllis Silverman

It becomes important to talk of the role of the professional. I am a very visible person. Director of this program is my job description and, at first glance, it is easy to conclude that it is essential to such a program for someone like me to be in charge. It does seem natural to be impressed and sometimes intimidated by credentials, but not necessarily appropriate, particularly with the awareness of the special value of widowed people helping each other, and it is this which we are trying to make possible.

To have a professional in charge, under ordinary circumstances, could mean the death of the program. It would not be mutual-help; that is, a program run by the widowed for the widowed.

My purpose, in this presentation, therefore is to help the widowed decide what may be asked from a mental health specialist, or from any other professional from whom they request assistance—either to consult with them in developing a working program, or to help them once they are underway.

At the very outset, I decided that, in order for our program with its special involvement as part of a medical school laboratory, to move toward self-help, I would have to define a special circumscribed role for myself. I knew that the tendency of a professional would be to take charge, run the show, and provide detailed direction as far as helping is concerned. If I did this, I would be setting up a professional agency, with the so-called "non-professional worker" in a subordinate role. I would not have a mutual-help organization. Insofar as it was possible to circumscribe my role, and to set the stage for us to become a mutual help organization, I think I succeeded. I will describe what I did.

I have been the link to Harvard and, to some extent, this has meant that I have "power" over the budget and the dispersal of personnel. As a result, I provided the program with continuity, stimulation and, sometimes, new ideas. To become self-help, however, these jobs need to be done by the widowed themselves. In setting up a structure for a new program, there must be the possibility of making the program continuous under widowed leaders who will most probably be doing this as volunteers on a part-time basis.

Since I was convinced that the widowed knew best how to help each other, I decided I could not tell any of the aides how to do their jobs. I had no reason to regret this. I often found myself awed by the soundness of their intuition about what troubles people. From their own successes and even failures, they bring a wealth of experience which they apply to helping others. This is the essence of such helping; from one's own life experience, one brings new perspective, hope and understanding.

We met regularly for discussions, questions and sharing ideas, which gave us a formal chance to keep in touch with each other. In between meetings, the aides called each other about what they were doing, and, perhaps, it was during these exchanges that the most important plans for helping individual widows emerged.

One of the ramifications of our getting together was to educate me. I was learning about what was involved in helping newly bereaved women and, as we moved on in time, what is required to help women who were no longer suffering from acute grief but who were learning to live as widows. For me, the challenge was to draw generalizations, to point to the implications of what the aides were telling me, and ultimately, to translate these into publishable articles.

The need to publish is unique to us, because we are a demonstration program in an educational institution, and when the value of what we were doing became apparent, we wanted to tell the world, to see the idea proliferate. I think the ability to pull together ideas, and to generalize from them, may be a quality professional training develops in an individual. One outcome of this is the written product. Another one, important to widowed groups and the professionals they work with, is that as a result of this ability, a professional can help to find common factors in the many situations in which they are involved. This helps to clarify and to see how what you decided to do in one situation can help you in another. (To some extent, informal get-togethers with each other provide some of this as well.)

I always have felt self-conscious talking to a widowed audience about my conclusions. Am I bringing coals to Newcastle? Betty Wilson has told me that this isn't true; most people don't conceptualize it for themselves and, therefore, they learn by seeing themselves in the whole picture. My training serves me well in developing this whole picture from all the many things that go on.

I have a favorite story of how I was educated. At the very first meeting, the aides and I had to plan the daily workings of the Widow-to-Widow Program. They were in complete agreement that it was not a good idea to visit before the woman had been widowed three weeks. They could not explain why this was important, but they felt sure it was the right thing to do. This, then, was the procedure which we adopted.

Two years later, a close friend of one of the aides became widowed. The aide was uncomfortable about visiting her right away. She thought she had nothing to offer, and that this woman would be upset by the fact the aide could now laugh and seemed fine; and could even wonder if she had ever felt as the new widow did now.

In my eyes, this observation was a negation of the entire basis of what we had been doing for three years. I immediately began to question why everyone so readily agreed and saw no contradiction in this. It seemed obvious to them, since they all observed that this woman did not as yet see herself as a widow. Until she did, she could not accept anything from another widow. In about three or four weeks things would change, they said, and at that point, the aide would become very important.

This, indeed, is what did happen. Then I was able to reflect back on this and we all agreed that the reason for waiting a period of time to visit was to give the widow a chance to acknowledge her new status. What has to happen is that she needs to realize that the word "widow" applies to her, even if it takes a much longer time to find out what this involves and to accept it psychologically and socially.

I cannot underestimate the importance of people who are working together in a service program meeting on a regular basis to talk over what they are doing. I was not aware of every person the aide visited, nor of the details in most situations. We talked about particular people who may have troubled the aide. What did I actually do then? The most important thing I did was give moral support, encouragement, and approval. I find I am asked to give *permission* to do things which they may see as correct, but about which they hesitate because they don't have credentials. The widow aides ask for corroboration of their assessments of people and their needs, in order to clarify their thinking as to how they best can help in trying to correct a specific problem. Sometimes I find myself making suggestions about how to approach certain situations. I often describe in detail how a professional psychiatric practitioner might approach the situation. These are primarily for the purpose of discussion, often set aside, rarely useful in any direct way, except to develop more information about the psychology of people in general. I don't expect these aides will follow orders and, therefore, I never give them. I have rarely had any reason to want to give such orders.

I think one of the most important things I do is give perspective; that is, show how the aides indeed are helping when things get discouraging. For example, when one woman was seeing only how the widow she was working with had not changed, and felt she was not doing any good, I pointed out that the widow had learned to drive and had obtained a part-time job. To remind the aide of this made her feel better, and she commented that it seemed that as long as the widow had someone to let it all out to, she appeared able to move ahead. It also was an opportunity for all of us to give the aide some moral support.

One of the things which came out in the workshop discussion was the need to help people to develop listening skills. In our experience, the people who do widow-to-widow work seem to have a natural talent for listening. In part, this comes out of an interest and curiosity about how other people feel. It also comes from a respect for others which says: "If I want to help, then I have to understand what they want and how they see it." It also involves learning to wait until asked to give personal examples, or until the other person is ready to listen. Maybe the group meetings have made the aides more relaxed and confident in what they can do and, therefore, they are able to listen, to wait, and to know that when they think they should do something, that's the time to do it. They also have learned from each other that there are some people who really don't want or need outside help.

One thing my professional colleagues always say is, "But they are untrained; they will get in over their heads." This has never happened. To help someone means to be involved with them, to care about them. To know how to live and how to cope with life's problems is not something we have any reason to believe a professional knows how to do any better than any of you. There were a few times when it was necessary to try to get a widow into psychiatric care and, in this, I tried to be helpful. However, clients have to go through a lot of red tape at an agency before they see someone. What agencies offer, for the most part, is the opportunity to talk with someone who may not understand as well as the widowed themselves what a widowed person is going through. In the time it takes to get into an agency, a widow or widower could be provided with the chance to talk, to think things out, and perhaps, solve some of his or her problems in the informal, friendly context of a widow-to-widow program.

In summary, let me say that there are two reasons why I think it is important to have a professional consultant working with the organization, or to have a professional advisory board. The first is to provide legitimation so no one can challenge the right to do this kind of work, and to help the professional community work with the mutual help organization and its members as colleagues. The second reason is the substance of this paper; that is, for moral support, encouragement and perspective about what is being done. A widowed individual who has developed experience as a helper can also do this latter job very well. As coordinators on the Line, Dorothy MacKenzie and Elizabeth Wilson do for the volunteers what I did for them in the Widow-to-Widow program. If they need additional advice, guidance or support *they* call me. There should always be this kind of back-up available.

A last word: remember you, the widowed, are asking the questions, and you *must* reserve for *yourself* the right to decide what to do with the answers and how you will use them.

Chapter X

PREPARING VOLUNTEERS

Throughout this book there have been references to how volunteers were trained, what took place at training meetings, and how often they were held. It seems appropriate to give this very important matter a chapter by itself, albeit a brief one, in which some of these details will be pulled together.

Part of the difficulty created for people beginning their own programs and who want to consider orienting volunteers has resulted from our philosophy that any extensive training program would make the volunteer too self-conscious and unsure of his own natural helping ability. We wanted him or her to be free to draw on his own expertise, developed as he or she coped with his own widowhood. Therefore, the primary purpose in any meeting prior to a volunteer's work with the widowed was to help that person see the relevance of his or her own experience as a widowed individual to what he or she would be doing in helping others; and to give information about agencies and other community resources which he or she might need to know about in the course of volunteer work. It would be better then to talk of a *preparation period* rather than a *training period* before the volunteer contacts other widowed individuals. It is essential to be a prepared volunteer whose special expertise comes from having been widowed—not a trained "non-professional."

Volunteers should be screened initially. In the Widowed Service Line, we developed an application form which asked about previous volunteer activities, work experience, experience in helping other widowed people, in addition to the usual information such as name, address, children at home, and time available to volunteer. In the group discussions, the participants agreed that a good volunteer is someone who knows how to listen, who is empathic and is willing to talk about her own widowhood. We feel that someone who is still very upset by his own grief is not ready to work in a widow-to-widow visit or a telephone line service. An initial chat with the future volunteer will establish the presence or absence of these qualities. There may be other administrative tasks they can do if they are not ready to help. One of the best ways to determine an individual's suitability is to let him participate in group orientation meetings. These serve to eliminate those who are not ready or unsuitable. The individual can often determine this himself after one or two meetings. There should be an understanding between the group and the new volunteer that there will be a trial period during which the new volunteer and the group can evaluate and determine the appropriateness of his continuing to volunteer.

In the original Widow-to-Widow program, the aides met with Dr. Silverman during this preparation period. In the Widowed Service Line, the preparation was provided by the program coordinators. Once there is a core of experienced volunteers, an outside individual does not need to conduct these preparation sessions.

We recommend that three meetings be held with volunteers before they see widows. They should attend two more meetings these after they begin helping. These should be considered part of this preparation period. The first three meetings can be held consecutively over a long week-end or once a week for two or three hours at a time. The following outline presents the series in perspective.

136

First meeting:

> The leader, in a round table discussion, reviews the
> needs of the widowed; why mutual help groups are ap-
> propriate ways of helping; what kind of help is needed
> and when in the period after the death of a spouse;
> what are the unique qualities of the help offered by
> another widowed individual. The participants are en-
> couraged to talk of their own widowhood as examples
> of the points made.

> A sharing of how the new volunteers became widowed
> should take place, how each accommodated, focusing on
> what assistance they needed and what resources were
> available or unavailable to them to give them any addi-
> tional help, noting how and what they learned that
> can be used to help others.

Second meeting:

> Continuation of the discussion of the first meeting;
> then going forward to talk about the community they
> live in, the death rates, and so forth, the health and
> welfare agencies that are available, and what kind of
> services, if any, they provide that might be of value
> to a widowed individual. There is a discussion of the
> referral process. There should be a review of financial
> benefits available and where these agencies are in this
> city. Each volunteer should have a folder with names,
> addresses, and phone numbers of agencies to which
> she can add new resources as they are discovered.
> They should also share with each other any comments
> on how these agencies work in reality, and what ex-
> periences they have in making referrals, or talking

with workers there, the focus being on whether they were helpful and, if so, in what way.

Throughout the year at regular volunteer meetings, representatives from various agencies should be invited to talk with volunteers about the services their agencies provide.

Third meeting:

Helping the widowed. In this session the volunteers begin to get involved in the mechanics of helping, how to contact the widowed, how to initiate a conversation, and they learn to feel comfortable as a helper by sharing initial discomforts with each other, and listening to the more experienced volunteers share some of their experiences to indicate how the process works, and what they had to offer. Sometimes role playing is helpful, sometimes just reflecting on how they would have felt had there been such a program, provides perspective.

Record keeping. This is discussed, so that the volunteers will have notes on whom they visited and can have easy access to phone numbers and so forth when they want to be in touch again. This is also important so that the organization can know whom it is helping and whom it is not reaching who may still need some help. There should be one volunteer in the group responsible for record keeping. He or she should have a copy of the record card the volunteer makes out. These are not for the purpose of keeping any confidential information on people who are helped, as one might find in a social agency, but simply cards with vital statistics like those found on death certificates that might be helpful for the volunteer to remember, such as children at home, who the widowed individual lives with, whether he or she is working, and so forth.

At the end of this meeting the volunteer should get an assignment; that is, the name and address or phone number of a widow or widower he is to contact before the next meeting.

If the group has not finished this business by the end of this third meeting, they may decide to meet for a fourth time before new volunteers contact a newly bereaved individual or return a call from a hot line. However, the volunteer should not delay in beginning to help beyond this fourth meeting. Otherwise, the orientation period becomes an end in itself, instead of an opportunity for "on the job training."

Fourth meeting:

Each new volunteer should have a chance to report on their first experience in helping, what happened, what needs became apparent, what they did and to ask any questions. Each volunteer should have a chance to talk for a few minutes and the group and the leader should discuss what happened. Another widow's or widower's name could be given to the volunteer if he has time and seems able to handle it.

Fifth meeting:

This meeting is simply an extension of the previous one. At the end of this time, the preparation period is over and the volunteer should be integrated into an on-going volunteer group that meets regularly to discuss its work.

Dorothy MacKenzie wrote the following description of the first three training sessions she and Betty Wilson conducted with new volunteers on The Widowed Service Line:

> It was very important for the volunteers to get to know us as people. There is a comfortable exchange of information about how we handled our widowhood; the sense of loss, the misgivings about returning to work, the problems encountered, and how we dealt with them. We got to know each other as human beings; our individual personalities and characteristics, likes and dislikes, and attitudes about any given situation all come to the fore at this time. Although we share the common bond of widowhood, we learn to deal with each other as individuals.

This opportunity to talk about their common situation of widowhood is very important. These are the experiences from which they will draw as volunteers begin to help other widowed people. Because of this, individual case examples of how help is provided are unnecessary. Each volunteer within herself, or himself, is an example of what needs a widowed individual has and what help he or she requires. The volunteer knows where gaps exist, what needs go unmet, and so forth.

The question most often asked by the volunteers during these first meetings is, "What will I say?" This is difficult to answer as there is no set formula when people have problems that run the gamut from extreme loneliness to wondering where the money will come from for next month's rent. Volunteers have to be encouraged to react as they would to a friend, or neighbor. As they accept the idea that they will be offering help they would offer naturally in everyday life, they seem to gain confidence in what they can do. There are some questions that the volunteers will hear often, especially if the widowed individual is newly bereaved: "When will I start to eat and sleep properly again? — Should I sell my house or move from my apartment; it's so full of memories. —Is something wrong with me if I want to go to the cemetery every day? or, I'm ashamed of myself, I never want to go to the cemetery. —My son always had good marks in school, but the other day he brought home a terrible report card."

The volunteers, who have experienced some of these dilemmas themselves, are not surprised by these questions, and they soon learn that this alone is reassuring to the widowed individual they are trying to help. The volunteer who is able to listen, to talk about what he or she did in similar circumstances, to present alternatives, helps the widowed individual find a direction that is appropriate to his situation. The preparation has to help the volunteer begin to feel comfortable in doing this.

It is important for the volunteer to know about community resources in the event that any special problems arise. For example, it has been our experience that very few callers need psychiatric care, but if it appears obvious that such help is needed, this is discussed with the widowed individual, and the volunteer needs to know what is available. The volunteers in general should be encouraged to call a coordinator or group advisor about any situation in which they have doubts about how to proceed, and if they feel that there is a potentially dangerous situation, additional guidance needs to be made immediately available to him. In our experience those agencies to which the most referrals were made were those offering vocational counselling and job placement, legal aid, and financial assistance. Volunteers were told to give widowed individuals the number of the information and referral service at United Community Services (Red Feather Agency) if they needed still more information about agencies. Volunteers could call themselves for the widowed individual if it seemed appropriate. It was also important to keep track of social groups for the widowed since many people asked about these after they had been widowed for some time.

At the end of this preparation period most volunteers will be ready to make a commitment. They should be asked to accept assignments for at least one year and agree to attend bi-monthly volunteer meetings. If a volunteer cannot attend at least one meeting a month, he should not be accepted. The meeting provides continuity and support. It also provides an opportunity for volunteers to learn from each other how to be more effective helpers. No volunteer is ever so expert that he cannot learn something new from these group discussions. In addition, he needs the moral support and friendship the group provides. He too is still experiencing some of the dilemmas of widowhood and his needs, in part, can be met in this way. In a mutual help program the volunteer can expect something in return.

PART III

Death, Grief, and Bereavement: The Professional Perspective

Introduction

These papers are included in this volume on mutual help for the widowed to give the reader an idea of the problems and attitudes of people, who in their daily work, serve the dying and the bereaved. Not only do these helpers need to understand the problems created by death but the people whom they serve should understand their perspective as well. If the widowed are indeed to be assisted in a more meaningful and efficient way, barriers between the professional and the layman or non-professional must be overcome. The clergyman, the physician, and the funeral director are all caregivers with whom any bereaved person must have some contact.

Traditionally, the bereaved, as the client or patient, is expected to accept the services provided by professionals without criticism. If he has complaints he usually keeps them to himself and becomes embittered and cynical. We propose that these papers serve as the beginning of a dialogue between these professional caregivers and the bereaved with the hoped-for consequences being the development of service more appropriate to real needs. The bereaved themselves should thus become active agents in planning, not simply the passive recipients of whatever happens to be available. For such discussion to take place, it may be the bereaved who have to take the initiative. Perhaps these papers will supply them with some background as the basis for initiating such discussion.

The perspectives represented here are those of a practicing sociologist, a physician, a clergyman, and a funeral director. They spell out some of the problems they face in their practice and explore some of the methods they use to cope with them.

Robert Fulton, as a sociologist, does his job well in providing an overview of the issues and their ramifications. His paper is really background for the papers that follow. He notes that as a result of the lower death rate, society now has a generation of young adults who have yet to face a death in their immediate family, and thus it is possible to call us a death-avoiding society. However, he notes that the population of widowed is increasing. In a mobile society such as in the United States, where family ties are weakening, these people face the possibility of a long life alone. There is an awakening interest among professional helpers, in how to help a person die with dignity and how to help bereaved families cope with their grief. Fulton documents the many developing programs that illuminate adjustment to bereavement as a legitimate area of human and scientific concern.

Melvin Krant, M.D., an internist and oncologist, writes with great feeling about the doctor's awkwardness in aiding a dying patient. He comments on the need to revise medical education so that the physician can relate to his patients throughout all phases of the life cycle. The challenge here is to find new ways of mobilizing additional community services and resources that assist the patient and his family in coping with this crisis.

Rabbi Earl Grollman articulates in a very personal way the dilemma we all face when talking about death, and facing our own mortality. He notes that clergymen are no more at ease with this than anyone else. More importantly, he talks of the need to help the dying patient *live* in whatever way he can until he dies, not to bury him in advance by isolating him in a sick room, and in a social situation where no one talks to him about what is happening to him or what is wrong with him. He points out the problem we all have in trying to comfort the bereaved, in finding the right words, and in really understanding their pain.

It is rare that we find a funeral director such as Sumner Waring who is able to describe the challenge in his work. We begin to see the conflict facing the funeral director who does a job few people would do—burying our dead. Because of this, he is often pictured in unsympathetic light. Waring points to the fact that while the funeral director buries the dead, he really serves the living. He notes the need to change and expand his training to serve more adequately those in real need, the surviving family. He also talks about how the funeral director can be helpful in developing Widow-to-Widow programs and offers some guidelines on how to obtain this help.

Chapter XI

SOME SOCIOLOGICAL OBSERVATIONS

By Robert Fulton, Ph.D.

The problems associated with death and bereavement are no longer the problems solely of the widow or widower. More and more, concerned professionals and lay people are beginning to appreciate the issues and difficulties associated with loss through death. While Dr. Phyllis Silverman is one of the pioneers with the Widow-to-Widow program in this country, she is by no means alone in her interest or efforts on behalf of the widowed. There is much evidence to suggest that a growing number of people across the country are taking up the public questions posed by these private tragedies. That this is so, is shown by the tremendous amount of information that is now available on the subject of death. In the last five years alone, more material has been published in the form of articles, research papers, speeches and lectures than has appeared in the previous 100 years. Recently, the Center for Death Education and Research compiled a bibliography of such materials. Through 1970, well over 1,000 such items could be listed, exclusive of theological treatises, religious tracts, or clerical sermons. It should be mentioned, moreover, that there are now in the country several centers specifically given over to research and education in this area. Dr. Robert Kastenbaum now at the University of Massachusetts, headed up the Center for Psychological Studies of Dying, Death, and Lethal Behavior at Wayne University in Detroit. Dr. Austin H.

Kutscher has established the Foundation of Thanatology at Columbia University, and at the University of Minnesota, we have a Center for Death Education and Research which is now in its second year of existence. Dr. Melvin Krant of Tufts University is in the process of establishing what is to be called the Equinox Institute, which will be devoted to exploring the social and personal meanings of death, dying, and bereavement in our communities. These various centers provide not only an educational opportunity for students to come to grips with these troubling issues, but they include off-campus programs for high school students and adults alike, as well as professionally-oriented seminars.

Basic fact-gathering is also sponsored by these centers, as well as the distribution of relevant information. At the University of Minnesota, we are engaged in a study of childhood bereavement as well as a study of the families of both living and dead donors who have or who are participating in the University's hospital kidney transplant program. In addition, an undergraduate course in the Sociology of Death is scheduled for the fall quarter, one of twenty such courses now being offered across the country at major American universities.

There are now two journals in the field—the *Journal of Thanatology* and *Omega*—both devoted explicitly to the issues and problems associated with death and dying in contemporary America.

Out of our experiences at the Minnesota Center, we have been made increasingly aware of the difficulties the dying and their families have in their relations with doctors, nurses, the clergy, and other members of the service professions. We have come to recognize, moreover, that there is a glaring lack of information and of basic social skills in this all-too-sensitive area. For the most part, medical practitioners and the clergy know next to nothing about grief and bereavement. The Widow-to-Widow Program is a most significant breakthrough in social and community relations in that it attempts to provide necessary help and assistance to the recently bereaved at the same time that it focuses attention upon their many problems.

But before I go any further with this line of thought, I should give you some basic demographic facts that bear directly upon, as well as help shape, the issues that concern us.

One out of every twenty people in the United States is widowed. There are almost twelve million widowed people in America today, of whom ten million (or almost 85%) are women. The majority of these women are fifty-five years of age or older. Many of them are first generation immigrants. They have limited formal education. They are the generation of women who did not work outside of the home. The majority of them today live on old age pensions, social security payments, or other retirement benefits, which are often inadequate, given the inflationary spiral of the last decade and the medical and other problems many of them have to face. It is estimated that over one-third of these persons are below the poverty line. Yet they have a life expectancy of still another fifteen or twenty years.

Progress in medical science and the enhancement of life generally in the past half-century has meant that the proportion of elderly persons in our society has increased tremendously. Ten per cent of our population today (twenty million pople) is over sixty-five. Moreover, this is an increasing population—the fastest growing age group of all. By 1975, it is estimated that twenty-five million people will be over the age of sixty-five. Basically, then, the problems that confront us today can only be expected to intensify in the years ahead unless we begin now to take corrective measures. Several national trends and cultural sets, so to speak, militate against an easy and ready adjustment to our burgeoning aging population and to the growing ranks of men and women who are bereft of their partners. One such trend is the emergence in our society of what sociologists call the nuclear family (i.e., a family that consists of only parents and children). We are less and less prepared to live with our grandparents (or other members of our extended family) today than formerly. Yet, while ideologically the country is in the process of becoming a two-generational society, demographically it is on its way to becoming four-generational. As mentioned, 10% of the population is now over sixty-five. It should also be noted that one-third of that group—three million people—are seventy-five years of age or older, with about 20,000 persons centenarians.

The upshot of this development is that many elderly persons now live physically removed from their children or grandchildren in various degrees of social isolation. Our society today, as you have heard so often, is indeed youth-oriented; there is a tendency to pretend that no one grows older than thirty-five nor, more importantly, *should* grow older than thirty-five. As a consequnce, there is a strong tendency to ignore or to avoid the elderly.

Added to the prejudicial "cult of youth" in America, is another development—secularization—that tends to deprive the elderly or widowed person of traditional community assistance. Today, half of the people in the United States are no longer church-affiliated; the priest or minister or rabbi is not the social resource person he was a generation ago.

Our society is also characterized by its high mobility; one out of five families moves every year. This leads to the breaking of old social ties, as well as to the reluctance to establish meaningful new ones. When death comes, people are often far from home and family.

These are just a few of the developments that make the problem of widowhood more acute now than in the immediate past.

A few more basic statistics should help us see these trends as well as permit us to understand more clearly the nature of the problem that we face. Seventy years ago, 53% of the deaths were of children fifteen years of age or younger, even though they constituted only 30% of the population. On the other hand, those over sixty-five made up 4% of the population and contributed 17% of the deaths. Today, those over sixty-five comprise 10% of the population, but contribute 66% of all deaths. Less than 6% of the deaths in American society today are of children under fifteen years of age. People, moreover, used to die at home. Today, two-thirds of all deaths take place in hospitals; this figure can reach 90% in some large metropolitan areas.

A death in a hospital, as I am sure many of you are aware, is a profoundly different experience from what it can be at home. For instance, the restraints placed upon the patients and their families and friends by hospital procedures and medical routines can serve to isolate and to separate the patient not only from his loved ones, but also from the medical staff itself. A study of nurses shows that, on the average, it will take a nurse twice as long to answer the buzzer of a patient if she thinks he is dying,

151

compared to her response to the buzzer of a patient she believes is on the mend.

In discussing a patient, nurses are known to use such terms as "vegetable" in reference to a comatose, or non-responding patient, or will refer to the patient who is dying as "going bad." When I was young, only apples and bananas "went bad;" people "died." Sociologists refer to such verbal behavior as "stripping;" that is, a process whereby the patient is reduced in his humanity and denied his identity in order to permit hospital or other institutional personnel to maintain control of their emotional reactions. The status of a patient is reduced further by hospital rules that limit visitation by adults and prohibit visitation by children without any compelling medical reason, and often in the face of a dying patient's over-riding wish to see once more a favorite granddaughter or nephew.

The modern hospital is also guilty of procedural rituals of deception, disguise and denial. In their middle-class haste to avoid a disturbance following a death as well as to suppress the fact, the medical staff often sedates the survivors shortly after they learn of their loss. Moreover, many hospitals go to elaborate means to disguise the fact that the patient has died. It has been reported to me that, in one hospital, bodies are "spirited" out in laundry carts in order not to "disturb" other patients. When "Dr. Blue" is called (the euphemism employed by hospitals when announcing over the loud-speaker systems that a death has occurred), the practice in many hospitals is for the nurses to commandeer the elevators and to position themselves at doorways and stairways to control the flow of people so that the body can be removed quickly, efficiently, and without detection, to the morgue.

One of the major problems that all of us face when we lose someone we love through death, is the hostility of our society toward the fact. Clergymen and doctors, we have discovered, are oftentimes the worst offenders.

Dr. Elizabeth Kubler-Ross has reported that when she first approached the medical staff of a Chicago hospital with the request that she be permitted to conduct her studies, she was startled to learn that, according to her colleagues, in the entire 600-bed hospital there was not a single dying patient. We live in an environment which looks upon the death of a person as a gross embarrassment; to die is a socially improper act—one which brings shame and causes discomfort to all concerned.

Probably the most extreme expression of the impulse to deny the necessity of biological death in our society is the cryogenic movement. Basically, the members of this association believe it is not necessary to die at all. Testimony to that belief is the fact that there are now twelve corpses lying in state in various repositories across the country, waiting for the day when medical science finds the cure for what killed them. By that time, it is believed, modern chemistry will have solved the problems associated with restoring a frozen body to life. It is appropriate that the motto of this movement is "Freeze; Wait; Reanimate." While these people like to believe themselves to be the ultimate secularists, I am prone to see them as practitioners of what I would term a "refrigerated christianity." What you should appreciate, however, is that these people may well represent the forward cutting edge of our secular, scientific-minded, materialistic society of tomorrow.

In such an environment, as the one I have just described, who is it that you can turn to when you are touched by death? Sad to say, there aren't very many people at all who are prepared to come to your assistance, either socially or emotionally. In fact, after the death, it is sometimes hard to find anyone who will even talk to you about your loss. What must be faced by the survivor is the fact that, in a very real way, he is confronted with a spoiled identity; as survivors we are stigmatized by the death of the ones we love. With one person out of every twenty a widow or widower, the problem that I just described is neither irrelevant nor inconsequential; rather, it is a very serious social problem with profound psychological overtones for us all.

But to whom can we turn? Some may turn to a clergyman or a doctor; some have relatives, friends or neighbors who are able to offer emotional and social support; others must turn to social workers and other active persons within the community who are able and willing to render what assistance they can. But for great numbers of people, the problem of finding the assistance needed at this particular time is exceedingly great and, as I pointed out the prospect is that this situation will become progressively more problematical as time goes by.

One person whom we haven't mentioned yet, but whom I believe can be of tremendous assistance at such a time, is the community funeral director. He, in most instances, is potentially capable of offering many different kinds of support and guidance immediately following a death. You should appreciate, too, that, like the bereaved person himself, the funeral director, by his close association with death, also suffers in his role from a stigmatized identity. In fact, it is my opinion that a great part of the hostility that has been expressed toward him over the past few years is traceable to his association with death itself, and is not a result of any basic cupidity with which he has been so often charged.

In this respect, I am reminded of a recent symposium in which the clergyman on the panel, a close associate of Dr. Kubler-Ross, upon learning that one of the members on the panel was a funeral director, announced to the audience amid uproarious laughter that while he was pleased to share the platform with a funeral director, he certainly didn't want his daughter to marry one. Prejudice aside, it is important to recognize that, in a study conducted at Langley-Porter Institute in San Francisco among families of children who died of leukemia, more than half of the family members participating stated that it was the funeral director who aided them most in adjusting to the fact and reality of their child's death. Apparently it was not the social worker, the psychiatrist, the staff physician, nor the chaplain, but the funeral director who, in facing directly the fact that a child had died, allowed the survivors to vent their grief—not disguise it—and in so doing, gave them an opportunity to come to grips with their personal tragedy.

What I think has to be appreciated is that the funeral director is as yet an untapped resource person in the community. He can be of vital assistance to you personally as well as to such efforts as the Harvard Widow-to-Widow Program. He is one of those persons whom we know can be of assistance to survivors. I would add, however, that your local funeral director may not now be willing or able to play this role as it needs and can be played. On the other hand, I think you can appreciate the potential for protecting or enhancing the community well-being that is inherent in his communal function.

Let me say in conclusion that this situation, as difficult and problematic as it is for adults, is even more so for our children. As I said earlier, young people don't die. The average life expectancy of a child born today is over seventy years. At the same time, today's child doesn't experience the frequency of death in his family or in his community as did his parents or grandparents. To the contrary—as an extreme example, I have a graduate nurse in my seminar who has yet to see a dead human body. While this may sound incredible to you, she has informed me that it is always her practice to close her eyes when faced with the prospect of seeing a corpse. Even at a family funeral only a few months ago, she reported to me that she was able to avert her eyes and came away from the funeral without ever having looked upon her dead relative.

In the vast majority of cases, men and women who are now twenty years of age have never experienced a death in their immediate nuclear families, while a sizable proportion of them have never attended a funeral. Paradoxically, while these young people have had little or no private or personal exposure to death, the mass media has presented them with a hostile world where murder and mayhem abound. It has been estimated that what might be called this first death-free generation, and which also may be described as the first TV generation, has (on an average) viewed approximately 12,000 homicides on TV since its introduction to this form of home entertainment.

The important question for us, is: How is that generation, in the face of this contradiction, going to react to the death of family members—to their grandparents, to their parents, to their brothers or sisters? How are they going to react to the death of strangers? How will they react to the prospect of their own deaths? These are questions, the answers to which will go far toward determining the kind of society they and their children will inhabit. I believe it is our responsibility now to see that the answers that they do ultimately find will be those that will contribute to the well-being of us all.

Chapter XII

SOME OBSERVATIONS BY A PHYSICIAN: CARING FOR THE DYING PATIENT AND HIS FAMILY

By Melvin J. Krant, M.D.

Some years ago it became obvious to me, working as I was in a cancer research unit, that it was an extraordinary experience being a physician to people who were dying. But it was also obvious that our group of physicians were paying little attention to the dying experience as a particular and singular event. I don't think I would be too crass if I said that our relationship with people who were dying was really based upon the concept that they were doing this as if to spite us.

The physician's role as a curing agent is directed fundamentally to the eradication of disease. A clinical research unit is especially conceived to develop tactics to prevent or delay death. If the patient does not respond to these tactics, we tend to find fault, either in ourselves, or in him. Our "protection," often was that if we failed, there must have been something intrinsically wrong with the patient. With many technologic successes under its belt, modern medicine has moved in the direction of more success, visualizing its destiny as a curing force, and not as a caring force. The fundamental attitude toward the cancer problem is: find the right biochemical, biophysical, technologic answer and the problem would all be over. Of course, in some regards, such an approach is quite correct. The eradication of cancer should not be disdained.

A number of years ago, I became uncomfortably aware that this was a rather short-sighted goal. Eventually all patients must still die, and I've been attempting to understand what the medical goal should be for the dying patient; and in that regard attempting to understand what dying means to those who continue living. That families have significant problems in dealing with issues of how to care for a loved one who is dying should be obvious. Yet the typical hospital setting seldom fosters explorations of perplexities as a unit, nor as single individuals, in relation to the patient, and in relation to the institution. What the meaning of the dying experience is to the living is not an issue in routine hospital practice, except perhaps where the patient is a dying child, and the needs of the parents seem to have some importance.

I decided to try to understand what human coping meant in regard to the dying-living relationship and what my role as physician in such an interaction could be. Is there a medical intervention role or is the matter a natural and private affair? Should we, and could we, participate in the events of losing before an actual death, so that recapitulation, growth, and restitution of life at some level, not ever the same as before, but nonetheless some level of continuation, could go on? The few things that I've learned about the dying-living process in this regard, are limited to cancer patients.

First, I have learned that predictions as to what the eventual death will mean to a family are not possible without lengthy exploration. People play "expected" roles and do not reveal their true feelings easily. Some people are significantly benefitted through a death. Caring for a sick family member has been too burdensome, and death is a relief. For some, death means the end of a bad marriage, or a bad relationship. Death may be interpreted as freedom.

Second, many family members go through a process of anticipatory mourning, which takes place long before death has occurred. In extreme cases we see families who stop visiting a loved one in the hospital, as if to declare that person socially dead long before biological and physical death occurs. These people are already reconstructing their lives before the loved one is even buried. I don't know really if they pay a psychological price at a later date for such behavior. I know that the patient may suffer inordinately when this abandonment occurs. There is also a bewilderment in the medical staff as they fail to understand why this kind of removal from proximity has occurred. Anticipatory mourning may be of benefit in the grief work, at least in connection with the period of disorganization immediately after a death, but this has yet to be documented.

Third, I think that the style in which people die strongly influences the manner that people grieve. There are people who seem to know that their dying should be a process of pride for their loved ones. They not only accept death, they enter into it with dignity and self-control. Such individuals may transmit strength to those who go on afterwards through an attitude and a posture in dying; it is as if they have something to teach the living, and the living do take pride in their strength. On the other hand, there are people who, when dying, seem bent on destroying everybody about them, through constant complaints and torments. The particular way of dying probably is of consequence for the manner and style of those people who will continue living.

Much dying takes place in hospitals, places usually poorly organized to care for the dying patient and his family. We could rule that birthing and dying are community home problems, and not hospital problems. But in fact they take place in hospitals or similar institutions today. Perhaps one of our jobs is to find ways of breaking down hospital walls. Perhaps the people involved in the caregiving for dying patients should be able to leave the hospital and come to the homes. As community-based caregiving in the form of general practitioners and others has diminished, perhaps the hospital has to become the center of community medical care-giving. In some ways, this sounds like home-care programs, but I conceive of it as something larger. The physician, the nurse, the social worker and others can be organized in the community to become natural care-givers for those who continue living as well as the dying. Such an organization, in which there is outreaching, is naturally involved in on-going programs after a death. It really isn't outreaching, as much as it's a natural setting event, a continuation of care to those who grieve but live on. This requires the teaching of what constitutes the work of grief and mourning to medical students, nursing students, social service workers, and all who participate in health-care giving, be they hospital based, or otherwise. Care of the bereaved can be seen as work in preventive medicine. Now there should be a place for non-professionals to work in such an arrangement, people who can play a part in a continued care-giving event both before and after a death has occurred.

There are many people in the community who are natural care-givers. They range from the next-door neighbor, who comes to cook meals for somebody, to the fellow who gets up a bit earlier to drive the kids to school when somebody else is sick. They include the druggist and the grocer on the corner. They're there to do something to help people through. A hospital-based program could integrate people in the community into linked health-care. Such a program might well help to re-integrate a community. I, personally, don't live in an integrated community now, and I think we'd be hard put to sell the urban-suburban proper American that the ideal dream of separate house, separate yard, and separate garage doesn't carry a terrible price with it— that the loneliness we seem to seek when we're alive and well becomes the kind of destitution we get when we're sick and in need. Since it is hard to have it both ways, we have elected, when possible, non-integrated, lonely areas of residence.

Another dimension is to create new institutions which can bring together community and the professional caregiver inside the walls of such an institution as St. Christopher's Hospice in London, England. It's a place created fundamentally to care for the dying in a community-style setting. The institution is far removed from the main central avenues of London, out in the suburbs. It exists in a rather sprawling, lower middle class community, and everyone about seems to know that this is a house of the dying. It's one of the most cheerful places that I've ever come across. It's very airy and filled with light, color, with sun, motion—all elements declaring something positive in the acts of living and dying. Four afternoons a week are volunteer days. Volunteers are invited to participate. The place is usually mobbed. The corridors are filled with people, almost bumping into each other, trying to be of help.

In talking to these people, their reasons for volunteering seemed quite varied. For some it was because they had participated in the loss of somebody in an institution that they thought could be run better. We are a death-bewildered culture, but I don't think we are a denying culture. St. Christopher's makes it evident that people of all walks wish to participate in people's needs, even dying patients, if they are given a formal structure to work in and an invitation to participate.

For many people, the dying of a loved one is a time of crisis. Given the fact that the dying patient is in the hospital, a professional staff can make this the time to institute a plan of intervention for helping a family meet the exigencies, psychological, social or religious, of that crisis. The loss of a loved one, or the process of going through a long, drawnout illness, engenders loss of all supportive societal functions, neighbors, friends, social organizations, community activities. The hospital can serve to bring multiple strengths in the form of doctors, ministers, nurses, community people.

Today, medical education, theological education, nursing education and the like, separate people rather than bring the various professionals together. The typical young doctor stands by the bedside, and the minute the minister appears at the doorway, runs right out, and says, "I'll see you later, you go ahead and do what you have to do now." We don't really teach what the community of living is about.

There is need to change medical schools so that they may become human life schools. The tradition of biological medicine should be maintained, but at the same time amplified. We must consider seriously bringing undertakers or morticians onto our hospital staffs, to participate in those events which actually occur around the final episode of life. Families should be brought together so that the different roles for carrying out the dutiful necessities when a death occurs can be rehearsed and planned before the death itself. The bewilderment that is faced by someone going into a funeral parlor to make burial arrangements, should be anticipated in the hospital setting *before* a death. There are a few hospitals which locate a funeral director as a part of the health care-giving staff, participating in helping the families cope with the bewilderment. Indirect benefits, such as improvement in the rate of consent to autopsy occur, because the mortician is seen as a natural participant in what the autopsy means, and can promise that the destruction of the body will not occur.

Physicians have no problems telling a family about the imminence of death. What is needed is guidance and counseling on the problems and meaning related to the death event itself. We can begin talking about autopsy even before somebody has died. We have to select to whom in the family we will talk. Different family members will play different roles in a crisis. Different people do different things, but there is always somebody less intensely involved, but who is still a family member who can begin to participate in some of these expected events by being taught and rehearsed what to do after. But no one in the family should be eliminated.

DISCUSSION NOTES

Much of the discussion at this workshop centered around ways in which the hospital cares for the dying patient, works with his family and deals with the dead. Primary interest seemed to focus on how to cope with the medical system as is, and how to make changes that would allow for better physical, emotional and spiritual care. It was noted that there is usually no room in which the family can wait and talk to hospital personnel about their sick member. Often they wait in hallways. The grieving family has no one to tend to their personal needs and problems, and they tend to be excluded from the care of the patient, to the point where the hospital staff will not permit them to see the body once the individual is dead.

Several people felt that there was value in viewing the body before the funeral director takes it. This helps to establish the fact that the individual is indeed dead. In the funeral home, he often looks unreal.

One funeral director talked of his own personal experience when his young child died in the hospital. They let the man, with his wife, quietly visit the body before they arranged for the funeral. The child looked at rest and it was very helpful to him as a parent to see the child in this way. As a funeral director he would recommend it as more common practice. One of the widow aides agreed with him, and reported that she often encourages people to ask the hospital to see the body and has done this with several friends. It is not helpful for everyone, but they should at least, have the choice.

One funeral director pointed out that there is less terror involved after the body preparation is finished and the body looks more natural. On the other hand, it is not possible to deny that the person did suffer. It is unreal to think that he should now look as he did many months ago before he became ill. There was consensus however, that the relatives should be given the option of viewing the body in the hospital, and that this could be helpful in accepting the reality of the death.

Families are often at a disadvantage in the hospital. It was pointed out that the head nurse can overrule the doctor by simply not informing relatives of his orders. Most families would not think to ask what are the written orders, or to call their physician to ask him to allow them to visit. Often the hospital staff alienate the bereaved because they do not know how to deal with death themselves. In some centers, there have been conscious efforts on the part of staffs to change and to be more aware of the human needs of the families.

The question was raised about the patient's right to know that he is dying and the doctor's involvement in being helpful about making a decision on this. There are some doctors who do not know how to give a fatal diagnosis. They rationalize that the patient will go through such agony by knowing that he will be destroyed or die socially. However, Dr. Krant pointed out, people often know anyhow. Some relatives, of course, do not want to tell the sick individual because they fear this news will cause him to lose hope or in some way precipitate death. Often the family feels that the patient should not be told because they sense the strain would destroy the family as they tried to deal with this information and with each other.

Dr. Krant believes that both of these decisions are open to exploration and both require that we attempt to understand why both the physician and the family members are taking this particular attitude. Almost invariably when it happens, enormous gulfs of separation are created between people at the very time when they need to be supported, to be guided, through a fatal illness. Dr. Krant suggested that these attitudes often have enormous consequences for the behavior of the bereaved afterwards. They may inspire anger, hostility, guilt and uncertainty—emotional stresses that insinuate themselves into those who must then continue to live:

It is not infrequent for families to come in with patients and to argue with me, saying, 'Don't tell so-and-so he's got cancer'; then you got to the patient's bedside and he tells you, 'Don't tell my wife I've got cancer.' These secret operations are never successful, and are always transparent, but playing out the secret becomes a way of living for everybody.

The discussion then turned to the question of who has the responsibility of telling the patient? An example given was a patient with whom the physician chose not to share the diagnosis, and who then begged to be relieved of this terrible burden of loneliness. Could the social worker or the clergyman tell him in spite of the doctor? Most typically in a medical setting this would be unheard of without an order from the physician. Dr. Krant pointed out that ordinarily there is such great respect for the doctor's authority in terms of what will help the patient physically that no one would dare challenge this.

One clergyman pointed out that he often can involve an individual in a discussion about his illness by joking about their both having an incurable disease. If the individual wants to talk, he takes this as an opening. He felt that many more people than we realize want to kid themselves and their families. Dr. Krant in some ways supported the position that the doctor should have the authority to decide what to tell his patient, and pointed to the dilemma created for the patient when he gets different messages from different people:

The individual is sick; he has put himself in the position of seeking help which puts him in someone else's hands and it is not easy to refute the hope that this individual stands for. When they become dislocated from normality, 99% of people are hopeful of being restored back to whatever that normality is. The first moment something goes wrong, we all expect and hope to be rescued— to get better. It takes a lot of time and effort to be able to work through for oneself the configuration that maybe 'I am not really going to get better after all.' The horror that can be created comes from the confusion fostered by someone saying one thing and your internal juices saying something else. An individual can get to the point where he says nothing rather than lose the little hope he has left.

It was noted that there seems to be a progression when an individual at first hopes he will recover, to the time when he knows he will not get well, to the hope that when the time comes he will not die alone and in pain. Dr. Krant agreed that it is very important to remedy current deficits in medical education and care for the terminally ill. He sees this change coming from those who have the leverage that comes with power—and this power at the moment is in the physicians' hands.

Dr. Silverman felt that these changes will be hastened if we combine our energies. She summarized the discussion:

It becomes clear that we have to distinguish between anticipatory grief that separates the family from the dying person before he is dead, and anticipatory work that helps the family plan openly and realistically for the death and assists them in facing the grief they will then experience. We do not want to reinforce denial. 52% of the deaths of young people are anticipated deaths. You've got an enormous population of people leaving surviving widows. These women are reinforced in a denial pattern which may make grief and any subsequent accommodation more difficult. In working with the bereaved, we have to help them get past this grief and denial before we can get to the real work at hand, which is building a new life. We need to help institutions change to be more open and to make anticipatory *planning*, not anticipatory grieving possible.

Chapter XIII

SOME OBSERVATIONS BY A CLERGYMAN

By Earl Grollman, D.D.

I have been asked to present the viewpoint of the clergy—
yet I cannot speak for all the clergy, nor can I even speak
for the Jews. They say that the only thing that one Jew
has in common with a second Jew is the agreement that a
third Jew should give to charity. So I will not speak for
all the clergy. I promise to speak honestly only for Earl
Grollman of Belmont.

It was Mark Twain who once said, "when a person
dies, we write the most unimportant information as an
epitaph upon the tombstone." What do we write? We
write the person's name, when he was born and when
he died. Twain said, "but what does this really tell
us about the person? Yes, we know the length of his days,
but we know nothing about the height of his aspirations
and the depth of his sympathies." And so I'd like to start
in a personal way; why I am interested in death and
bereavement. What is my approach? What are my aspirations?

I come from a Baltimore, Maryland family, where the
word "death" was never mentioned. This may parallel
some of your own experiences.

I graduated from the university and then went to the
seminary where I was ordained. Despite the fact that I
was a rabbi, I must confess I knew very little about the
psycho-dynamics of death except how to write a eulogy
when a person died. The first time I attended a funeral

171

was July 1, 1950 when I became assistant rabbi at Temple Israel. I'm not sure if it's true for the Protestant and Catholic clergy, but as soon as the assistant comes, the senior rabbi goes away on vacation.

It was July 1, 1950; I was sitting in my new office in Temple Israel, the telephone rang, and somebody said, "Is this Rabbi Grollman?" I wasn't sure; the name sounded strange, but I said, "Yes" in the kind of phony voice that I thought was the way we should speak.

The person went on, "I have such terrible news, we have a twelve year old son who just drowned at summer camp in Maine." This was my first real experience with death.

In the years that followed, death did not remain a stranger. I have witnessed joy and sorrow, friendship and bereavement, yet I can say this to all of you, there is a difference between officiating at a funeral of an elderly person whom you don't know, and that of somebody close to you—either a member of the family or your closest friend. This is really one of my great difficulties in being a rabbi: what happens when you become intimately involved. You know the person, and you want to stand up and become the mourner; instead you are the officiator.

I had a close friend in my congregation; I saw this strong, virile man become sick, afflicted with cancer. He died on a Sunday evening. When the telephone call came, I went immediately to the family and they didn't say "Rabbi Grollman," or "Dr. Grollman," they said, "Uncle Earl, what do I do? What do I do?" I really didn't know and I thought, in tribute to this person, whom I truly loved, I vowed that I might understand more about death and help others in bereavement.

172

Some Observations by a Clergyman

I had worked within the fields of psychology and religion but it was mostly theoretical. I wrote a book dealing with Sigmund Freud; I had been interested in existentialism, but I wanted to do something that could help people in their day-by-day pursuits. I went to the Widener Library at Harvard University, and I saw all kinds of articles dealing with death and children, but they were entombed in professional journals. I continued taking graduate courses at the Boston University School of Theology, with an emphasis upon death and bereavement reactions. As a result, I edited a book called *Explaining Death to Children,* an anthology dealing with the subject from the Jewish, Catholic, and Protestant points of view, as well as from sociological, psychological, and anthropological prospects (Grollman, 1967).

I wanted all the gatekeepers and especially clergymen, to be aware. I must mention a book that some of you may have seen, called *Conflicts of the Clergy,* written by Margareta Bowers, a psychiatrist. She says that one of the reasons a person enters the religious field is because he himself is afraid of death. By becoming a minister, he is in charge of death; he has autonomy over it. Very often when you investigate his life, you will find that there had been a death in the family with unresolved grief reactions. By becoming a minister, he walks in and takes charge (Bowers, 1963).

I think clergymen very often mishandle death. Often the clergyman says, "I'm so afraid of death," or the Catholic priest might say, "I officiated at the funeral of my mother, and it just destroyed me that I had to be the celebrant instead of a mourner." A close friend of mine was a professor at Boston University School of Theology. One time he talked in terms of the death of his own wife, and he said, "The funeral was an abomination. The officiating minister kept talking about how lucky she was to enter into a better life."

My friend continued, "Damn it, it may be a better life for her, but it's not a better life for me." He had viewed the funeral not as the officiant or clergyman, but as a spectator. It was no longer efficacious and meaningful.

I think that very often when we deal with children, as well as adults, we, as clergymen, say the wrong things. We feel that we have to say something profound or that we must talk in the language of the Bible, rather than talking in terms of the life of the deceased and the needs of the survivors. When the clergyman walks in, and perhaps he's speaking to the boy whose father had died, he might say, "Your father died because he was a good man, and God takes those who are good." (Have you ever heard this before?)

Remember the movie, *Yours, Mine and Ours,* with Lucille Ball? In the opening scene, Lucille Ball is portrayed as a widow. Her husband has just died, and her little boy is acting up all over the place. And Lucille Ball says, "Why are you so naughty?" And the lad retorts, "Because you said God takes those who are good, and I don't want God to take me." I think the next question is, "If God takes those who are good, what are you 'mamma', doing here?" Sometimes we say, "Your father is now up in heaven." Now I'm not against the word *heaven*. But I think that we must explain this word to the youngster and be prepared for those interrogations. If "father is up in heaven," then why are you burying him in the earth? And we know of cases of children in airplanes who

174

look up in the clouds (in heaven) seeking their deceased loved one.

Very often in our desire to give easy explanations, we bring confusion and consternation. I've heard clergymen say, "Your father is away on a long journey." The child might think; If he's "away on a long journey," why is everybody crying? The greatest fear that every child has is the fear of being abandoned. All of you who have small children might recall that when you would leave them even briefly they would cry. For them, it seemed like abandonment, death.

Or very often we say, "Your father is now asleep." Now I've read *Homer,* and I've read the *Iliad,* and *Thanatos,* and *Hypnos;* sleep and death are twin buds of the same flower. But I have known children who are afraid to go to sleep at night because they can't distinguish between real sleep and eternal sleep. I think that funeral directors, make a mistake when they call some of the rooms "slumber rooms." The person is not asleep; the person is *dead,* never to return on this earth.

I find that when I speak to young people and to older people that it is inordinately important that I not explain to them what I believe, but instead try to understand what they think. For example, I recall a television appearance which I was to make. In preparation, I asked some of the younger students of my religious school to quiz me. I said, "Death is permanent." And a little girl said, "So what?" I said, "Permanent!"

She said, "My mother has permanents; how long does a permanent last?"

Dealing with death is the most important aspect of my entire ministry. It's the one time I am really a minister;

it's one of the times that I am really needed. The telephone rings, I answer and somebody says, "Rabbi Grollman," and then there is a sob, and I know what's going to come next. No matter what is occurring, I usually say, "Where are you?" And when I do seem them, I find that the best approach is non-verbal. It is not one of verbosity, but rather of touch. I walk in and embrace the survivor. And guess what I'll say? Nothing.

I think so often we have the compulsion, especially we who are clergymen, to bring in some kind of magical formula. "It's God's will." I've heard so much garbage uttered in a house of bereavement. People believe that they have to say something abstruse. "It's God's will," and you look around, and who's the person who's saying it? It's an atheist. How do you know? She says, "Honest to God, I'm an atheist."

I will take the person's hand, sit down, and listen. Usually I hear something like this: "Here I was, and he said, 'I'm not feeling well,' and I rushed over to him, and he fell down and I went to pick him up, and I got him a glass of water, and I called the ambulance, and . . ." She goes over and over and over it again. I listen, and then somebody else walks in the room and she tells the same story again and again and again. What is she really doing? She is trying to say, "I don't believe it's really so." Or, "I really did everything that was possible." She is trying to exonerate herself in terms of guilt and recrimination.

As a clergyman I have other responsibilities. When a death occurs, very often their mother will say to me, "Will you tell the children?" My answer is "no." Is that callous? I say, "I will be with you, but we must all be together as a family unit."

Also if it is the father who has died, I advise the mother not to tell his young son that he is now the man of the family. He is *not* the man of the family. I have seen too many cases where the boy actually wants to take over the role of the father, even to the extent: "Can I now sleep with you?"

I tell the children that it is permissible, if they desire, to cry. Tears are a tribute of yearning for a person who has died. I am unhappy with the sterile approach at funerals by some clergymen who say, "Don't cry, you've got to be strong." That's nonsense. Somebody has died, and when a person dies, part of you has died with this individual. I tell the family, "If you want to cry, cry." Sometimes the youngsters are seemingly unmoved at the death. The children might say, "Oh. Can I go out now and play?" I try to explain to the survivors that it does not mean that the child did not love the departed loved one. It is so sudden that he just cannot accept the reality of death. When a child says, "Can I go out and play?" this is his way of fending it off; this is part of his mechanism of defense, of denial.

Most of us deny death. The finite mind does not accept finality so quickly. Those of you who are part of the Widow-to-Widow program tell me that even after the funeral is over, when the telephone rings you unconsciously think, "Maybe it's my husband." Or, if the deceased had been in the hospital for a length of time, you begin driving there after work almost automatically. We do not accept the fact just because we are told somebody has died; the mind accepts this reality very slowly.

Very often the parents will say, "I don't think I should take the child to the funeral, do you? I mean, after all, I don't want to expose him." My answer is, "Why don't we find out what the child thinks?" In my book, *Explaining Death to Children,* at the age of 7, I felt a child should be able to attend a funeral. However, I now realize that no one can arbitrarily set a chronological age level. You cannot state that at a certain age a person can be present at a funeral. Certain criteria should be present. First, I think the children should know what a funeral is all about. It is unconscionable to take a child to a funeral if he does not know what is going to happen. This is one reason why I wrote a book called *Talking About Death for Children* (Grollman, 1970). When my children went to the hospital to have a tonsillectomy, we would take out a little book called *When Johnny Goes to the Hospital.* But when they go to a funeral, it is shrouded in mysticism. Clergymen have a responsibility to speak to the children and explain what a funeral is.

We have a funeral director come into our temple and explains to the youth what they might expect in terms of caskets, funeral homes, and embalming. As a clergyman, I sit down with the family and explain the procedure.

Secondly, I try to elicit from the young person himself whether he wants to attend, not making him feel guilty if he prefers not to attend. The decision is his. Very often the parent will say, "You don't have to," which means, "don't go."

Another aspect of my role as a clergyman is to help the family to formulate the funeral arrangements. In my own congregation, I make the original call to one of the funeral chapels, to one of the funeral directors. The family often just doesn't know what to do. It's amazing to me, especially in my congregation which is made up largely of professional people, that they are completely in the dark about these procedures. This is true even when there is an imminent death; they refuse to think about a burial plot.

It is equally important, to be concerned with the family before an individual dies. Of late, I have become concerned about the terminal patient. I recall one night when I was working in a home for runaway children, I had a miserable experience with a young girl on LSD. As I was driving home, I decided to visit a member of my congregation who was dying. I thought, "I may as well, it is on the way." I walked in about 7:30 in the morning, and said stupidly, "Hi, how's everything?" And he said, "What's wrong? I can tell by your voice."

And I told him exactly what had occurred the night before. For an hour I talked; I just had to unburden myself. He turned around, sat up, and faced me and I suddenly realized that we tend to treat a dying *patient;* we forget he's a dying *person*. What I do now in terms of the dying *person* is that I spend time working with him, finding out where he is; what his needs might be. I feel that I am a more effective counselor and clergyman as a result.

It is then important to ask in what way it is possible to help the family prepare in advance for the fact that they're going to face a funeral in a month or two weeks. My experiences in my own community have not been what I've been reading in the psychiatric journals. The technical phrase they use is, anticipatory grief, in that you anticipate death and work it through before the funeral. My own experiences do not reinforce this theory. On the contrary, even after a long illness, I find that the survivors have a difficult time adjusting to the reality of death.

I make an attempt to get people to talk about actual plans about the funeral. In Judaism we have a worship called *Yiskor*. The service is devoted to the dead, yet many worshippers, at this time in the service used to leave, with only those who have been bereaved remaining. I have indicated that this is an opportunity to talk about death; the processes involved, that all of us must face the inevitable—now everybody remains. When somebody is terminally ill, I say to the family, "I don't know and it's not in my hands, how long he will be living. But I can tell you this, that when it does occur, it's really so difficult in one day to make all of the arrangements. The time to plan for the inevitable is now."

The problem is that if the family buys a funeral plot they fear superstitiously that he may die earlier. One of the mythologies in Judaism is that you do not name someone after the living, at least in the Orthodox Ashkenazic tradition. One of the reasons is that even Angels of Death make mistakes. If I have a son by the name of Earl Grollman, and the Angel of Death comes to take Earl Grollman, Sr., he may take little Earl Grollman, Jr., by mistake; the younger one for the older. If a person is very sick, some change his name "alter" or "old," or they change it to "Chaim" which means life. It is to confuse the Angel of Death.

In terms of the funeral, it is my responsibility as a clergyman to make sure that the burial plot is not left to the last moment. Also I have to ascertain if the family wants a eulogy. I believe in the eulogy. I believe that the funeral is not for the deceased alone; it is also for the living. One of the techniques that I find to be uniformly successful in obtaining information for the eulogy is to say, "I didn't know your father too well, so any information you can give me will be helpful." I always make sure that at the funeral I don't say "the most," especially since I heard of a rabbi who said, "He was the greatest husband," only to find out the man had a coronary while sleeping with another woman. I try to find something which I think might be true and keep it in a low key. I go to the house of bereavement and speak to about three different people and if these three people will use the same word, such as "gentle," you have a pretty good idea that the guy was probably gentle. In this way, the eulogy is not only sincere but honest.

In many of our services, the rabbis read some prayers which are not always appropriate. I think that the funeral will go through some kind of transformation just as the wedding service has, where young people are helping to write their own wedding services because they want them to be relevant. What we need now is to have some kind of funeral service which meets the needs of the people.

I have to tell you of a recent experience when a little child in my congregation died. You can imagine the hysteria at the funeral service. There were shrieks and yells and screams, and I began reading, "The Lord is my Shepherd." I didn't know what these words really meant, especially in these circumstances. The family who had many other children, from six on. They all attended the funeral as a family unit. (Children feel abandoned and the more they can participate rather than being shunted aside, "You go and play with your friends", the more they feel that they're part of the cohesive group process). As I was officiating, I discovered that no one was really listening. I surprised myself by leaving the pulpit, standing in the front row of the chapel and speaking to the children. Suddenly everybody began to listen.

As clergymen, we must find out what will be meaningful to the family. For example, is there a poem that is meaningful? Instead of just picking up the clergyman's manual and using it as our *only* guide, we certainly have to supplement it. After the service is over, we go to the cemetery; I think that more and more people are trying to avoid this procedure. Yet this is the moment of truth. I believe in the funeral because it gives a climate for tears, a climate for sharing, a climate to dispel denial.

I think that physicians sometimes make a great mistake at funerals. Every time somebody cries, they give the survivors tranquilizers. Sometimes the mourners are so anesthetized they don't realize what's going on. One mechanism of defense is denial according to Anna Freud. "I don't believe it, tell me it didn't happen, it's a bad dream and I don't believe it." It doesn't mean that we still won't fantasize and say that maybe he is coming back. The funeral says that the person is dead, never to return. The moment of truth is when you stand at the cemetery and there is the casket and there is the hole. You can say whatever you want; he's not away on a long journey; he's never coming back, at least during this earthly pilgrimage.

After the funeral is over, is when my work really begins. The movie *I Never Sang for My Father,* ends with this statement, "Death ends a life, but not a relationship." But people still have to continue on, and there are the 'nitty-gritties' to work out. I make it my concern to continue to see the bereaved people; not just once. Many clergymen make a condolence call; they run in and run out, or they'll conduct a service, because it's easier to conduct a service than to speak with the people. I make sure that I visit at least three times during the week of *Shivah* (mourning period after the funeral), but I don't go in the evening; I usually visit early in the morning. It's the time they are really able to talk and they want to talk; it's the time when very few people are around and I listen to the people. It's what Sigmund Freud called the "sighs of dissolution."

I'm shocked when I walk into a house of bereavement, although I used to do the same. People talk about everything except the person who died. You know, "The Red Sox beat Detroit yesterday, we're 2½ games . . .". "Let me tell you about my golf game . . ." everything, except about the person who died. This is my opportunity to come in, not to pontificate but to try to understand where the person is. I remember one time coming in and saying, "I'm awfully sorry." And the person said, "I'm glad the bastard died."

There are all kinds of feelings that I'm sure you have discussed. One is idealization. A cartoon appeared in a recent *Sunday Boston Globe*—two men were talking. One says, "There's no such thing as a perfect person," and the other man said, "There is—my wife's first husband." This whole idealization goes on—"He was so great and wonderful." I let the person know that the deceased was human, not that I cast aspersions or undermine his character. He was a human being and the more the mourners are able to to talk about the frailties, the more they're able to understand the person who did die.

It is not the expressions of these feelings that are dangerous, but rather the suppression. For example, there are feelings of anger. How do widows usually talk about their husbands? "When he left me." Right? "When he left me." As if it were an act of volition and sometimes they'll say, "It's easy for him. He's at Sharon Memorial Park (a cemetery), but me, I have to worry about the children" and I hear people say, "Don't say that." As a clergyman I tell the survivors, "You say whatever you want. Whatever comes to your mind is acceptable, just be yourself. This is acceptable to me, just be what you need to be." There are so many emotions concerning death, anger, and yes, projection of guilt. Very often I will hear somebody say, "The doctor killed him." Did you ever hear this? Now, I'm sure doctors make their own mistakes, but this happens so often when you know it's a terminal case that the doctor could not be culpable. They're really trying to say, "I had nothing to do with it, I am not responsible, somebody else is." Or very often, I, as the rabbi, become the culprit. I will never forget one of the first funerals that I conducted in my community. I had been there for just a few months and knew the family, yet when I walked in the house after the death, they said, "Get out." I didn't understand; then I realized that I was the surrogate of God. You can preach on a Sunday morning or Friday night and say, "Thus saith the Lord," but when you walk into a bereaved family they say, "Dammit, why did *you* kill him?" The antagonism and hostility also may be directed towards the funeral director. He becomes the representation of death, and the foil for their feelings of projection of guilt.

As a clergyman, I speak in terms of forgiveness. God forgives you, but will you forgive yourself? I think the whole idea of forgiveness and our religious resources can help to soften some of these people who are so burdened by this tremendous amount of guilt and recrimination. And I find, especially with children, the guilt is tremendously great, because children believe in crime and punishment. If a child does something good, we say, "Ah, you're a good boy, you can watch television tonight." Or, "You've been bad. You don't go to the movies on Sunday." So I discover that when death happens the child begins to think in his own mind, "What did I do wrong?" A child thinks in terms of the omnipotence of words. "One time . . . I said, 'drop dead'." He thinks because he said "drop dead," that this is why it happened. I try to work with the child, and also with the parent, (because parents are really children, only they're more sophisticated). Wishing doesn't make it so; the person died for lots of reasons.

I try to allow the person to walk through "the valley of the shadow." As a clergyman I believe (and I represent the liberal wing), in customs and ceremonials dealing with death. To carry out traditions and ceremonials related to death is also saying, "I didn't do everything I could in life, but I sure can do it now." In my congregation, there are people who come to the Temple every single morning at 7:00 to say the mourner's prayers as is prescribed in Jewish Law for the entire mourning period (11 months). As I counsel them and work with them, I find that many of these people really feel guilty. By going to the Temple they're doing something at the time of death which they did not always do during their loved one's life. In addition, they hear from others: "Isn't he a wonderful son," because of the fact that they come each morning. Customs, ceremonials, and traditions do help us in times of adversity. It was Margaret Mead, who said, "When a person is born we rejoice, and when they're married we jubilate, but when they die, we try to pretend that nothing has happened." Customs and ceremonials give us some kind of drama, as well as a link with history.

I conclude with something of my own tradition. A Chasidic 'rebbe,' an old Orthodox rabbi, was told by one of his disciples, "I love you." The rebbe said, "Do you really love me?" When the student said, "Yes," the rebbe said,

"Do you know what gives me pain?" And the young person said, "How do I know what gives you pain?" The old Orthodox rabbi replied, "If you don't know what gives me pain, you don't really love me." As a clergyman, death and bereavement provide the time I am really the clergyman; it's the time I share resources; it's the time I really have the opportunity to understand the person—not only in joy—but in sorrow.

Chapter XIV

THE ROLE OF THE FUNERAL DIRECTOR

By Sumner James Waring, Jr.

I come to you as a practicing funeral director and as a trustee of medical care within a community where I serve on the Board of Trustees of Truesdale Hospital, Fall River, Massachusetts. Of course, the challenges of increasing hospital costs and the limited number of modern rooms within these hospitals are with us. The 'preventive medicine' concept of minimizing the patient's need to be admitted to a Medical Care Center until it is an absolute necessity weighs heavily in considerations from which plans for future medical care in our Area evolve. Hopefully, pursuit of this sort of 'care-giving' policy will maximize the value of the patient's 'care-buying' dollar.

When we think about funeral service and its interrelated effects upon the people concerned, we also recognize need for some preventive 'medicine.' There is need for our profession to communicate with the general public prior to need; not for the purpose of persuading them to spend more dollars than they can afford, as our occasional detractors would like you to believe, but to approach them as counselors; giving them some exposure, some reassurance, some familiarity, in a very gentle way, with what might have to happen before it comes to the point where it isn't so gentle. For example, the disclosure of a malignancy, or of a limitation due to a heart condition, or the time when a death has actually occurred, are not good times for carefully thinking through funeral plans and arrangements.

The functions of my particular profession appear to be grim, quite 'funeral' in the eyes of the average layman, and therefore distasteful. An individual's death-denying impulse makes this quite understandable. Actually we serve and deal with the living who most always love that life which has been lost, and who must now cope with disposing of that loved one. True, our public health function directs us in our responsibility for professional care of the deceased. However, the overwhelming majority of our hours are devoted to serving the living . . . and it is to this end that our firms are staffed and our personnel trained.

By nature, the funeral director has always been a counselling friend, with the importance of this function being intensified by the needs of contemporary society. However, funeral service for many years emphasized the technical skills involved in preparing the body. There are certified mortuary colleges, such as the one at the University of Minnesota which grants a degree in Mortuary Science. Unless the funeral director receives his training at such an institution, and more and more of the younger men are, he is likely to be trained only in the technical work. In the last decades, there have been great advances in our knowledge about problems created for the survivors by a death in the family and in the developing of counselling techniques to help them more effectively. Aside from his personal ability developed from years of experience, the funeral director has not been trained as a counsellor. As a counselling profession, the funeral service finds itself in a virgin field. Clergymen and physicians are experiencing similar problems. Their technical training always has been quite advanced, but they are finding from experience the very real need to learn to deal more effectively with peoples' emotions and life problems. As training centers for funeral directors are beginning to introduce courses in the psychology of grief and grief counselling, so the clergy are developing programs to bring clergymen in contact with the dying patient. Andover-Newton Theological Seminary has one program I am aware of; they place clergymen at Boston City Hospital. Not only do the chaplains learn about people dying, but they see them and feel them dying. It's an earth-shattering experience for many of them; as earth-shattering as for the embalmer who for the first time holds a heart in his hand.

Physicians who get used to death because they see it all the time are very direct with people about the problem. This direct approach may be cruel to some of us, but in many ways the physician does people a real service if he approaches death this way. Everything else would be a little easier, in spite of its ugliness, if this is handled well.

I would define our role as "coordinative." We, together with the clergy, function usually as the prime care-givers during the period immediately after a death. We must handle everything just as those who place their trust in us would like to have had it handled were they free of grief, and totally familiar with necessary decisions and involvements. We must offer our advice in a manner which will cause them days, weeks or months—maybe even years— later to say, "They did everything just as I would have wanted had I known what to do . . . had I not been so upset." The clergy with whom I work are extremely conscientious and cooperative. Their door is always open. I think this word cooperation goes right along with coordination. We professionals, the clergy, the physician, and the funeral director, have to enjoy common appreciation and respect for each other's intentions and capabilities as we experience the dynamics of today's life-style. Directing this regretful, but very real happening through the right door when there is need for one of these doors to be opened is the very real responsibility of *all* including well-meaning friends. We guide those we counsel through the grief-funeral experience in a manner which is respectful of, and thus in tribute to, the life lived by the deceased. We try to respect the accepted guide-lines of burial in both the contemporary and traditional sense excepting the few cases where such is not one's faith, or desire. We always allow for, and encourage personalization of each individual funeral service with accompanying right to incorporate 'change' while respecting the generally accepted custom of the society in which we live, and carrying through our public health responsibility as defined within the guidelines of our particular locales.

It is really the living we are serving, not the dead. The technical application applies to the deceased. Death may be sad, but a funeral can be something that emphasizes life (like the new Catholic Mass). These are living people, perhaps more alive than ever in the sense that all segments of the emotions are working. We have to sense the individual's needs and make the situation one to help him through the experience of grief. Here's where our co-ordinative function comes into use.

For instance, the funeral director can explain to the widowed all about their Social Security benefits. He should check back later to see if the bereaved have done something about it. If not, he should take them by the hand and help them to make sure they get there; some firms provide a car for this purpose.

Dr. Silverman said she expects that we can tell who might be going to have some trouble—we certainly can.

We develop a feel for it. Some people can make it on their own; others seem very independent at the time of the funeral but sometimes we sense that this is a cover and know that in six months or so they may fall apart. Ideally, we should provide some follow-up. This follow-up, this caregiving role is one that is the real challenge. However, as I said, we have a lot to learn and we do not always have the time and the facilities to follow through. If we were to incorporate this kind of service, there would have to be a total re-evaluation of the funeral director's present functions and priorities.

There should be a Widow-to-Widow program or something similar in every community. The funeral director will know many people who could use this kind of help, and in this way provide additional guidance for the bereaved he serves. He could have a "visiting friend" on his staff . . . someone who could find a way of reposturing himself for this service. I would like to see this happen, but we have a long way to go.

Let me give you some examples of the kind of situations in which we become involved; the range of human problems we meet as practicing funeral directors. First, there was the young man and his wife who lost twin babies, pre-mature births, six months along the way. This fellow was allowed by his physician to touch the youngsters when the babies were in their incubator. It was the most tender bit of thinking, and most apt bit of insight I've been exposed to recently. That obstetrician was one well-trained physician. All that father talked to me about after their death was the fact that he had been able to see and touch those babies. The fact that they had gone became a little bit more acceptable because of this. It was a real comfort, and he was able to come with me to some really sound

decisions regarding how this death would be treated, what
the tribute would be. This particular tribute happened
to be a cremation, and the scattering of ashes onto the
shores of the Atlantic Ocean. It was quite an experience
for me, needless to say.

The next instance is of parents who lost a youngster
who was through her teenage years. She had been dying
since about the age of nine or ten. The parents knew this
was going to happen, but they had been fighting it. I don't
think anyone had really been able to help them come to
grips with it. It happened under bad circumstances, however. The youngster was up the night of her death, she
took nourishment, she walked around her room with her
parents and they left around 8:00 at night. At 11:00 that
night they were called; she had convulsed and died. I was
called to the house and you could feel the thickness of
that air. The clergyman hadn't yet been able to get close to
that situation. Here is one of those bereavements which
we could feel is going to be bad. It is bad, and it's going to
get worse before it gets better. But the community was helping; during visiting hours at the funeral home, the group
sharing of their grief was very, very helpful to them. You
could just watch it start to help them. Emotions were bare,
and it was quite an experience to see all the reactions.

In another instance, a man died leaving his second wife
and an only daughter from his first marriage. At his
death, the daughter and the second wife clashed, evidently
as they had through his life. When it came time to take care
of the funeral arrangements, the daughter, on one hand,
told me the stepmother was unreliable. On the other hand
the stepmother told me the daughter tended to be the flam-
boyant type. When we were making arrangements, if one
agreed, the other automatically disagreed. It was impos-

sible. Finally we threw out all the alternatives so we could begin at a point where they might agree. When the selection of the casket arrived, neither would volunteer a choice because each wanted to make the second choice in opposition. It was very obvious what they were doing. If they could ever have resolved their differences, we would have hoped it would have been through their shared experience of grief. But it didn't seem to work out.

We see people at the most difficult periods of their lives. We respond to these needs from our experience, from our training and with all the resources we have as human beings. You can see why, in the face of this range of human emotions, we need to find more and better ways of being helpful.

I would like to comment now on one factor which I consider to be most important. This is the financial implications of the funeral. At times it becomes convenient for our detractors to project the costs of funeral services as unreasonable. I shall simply state that they are not!! It must be made perfectly clear that I know of no funeral director in this land who wouldn't accommodate the most modest desires, or capabilities of the people they serve. Also, however, it must be recognized that we are affected by the inflationary spiral. The conscientious funeral director who is worthy of your confidence in the first place, will staff his firm with personnel possessing the sort of character and reliability which generates a feeling of comfort when you entrust your loved ones to his care. Licensing requirements within funeral service call for certain educational qualifications to be satisfied. Our personnel must be subject to "call" twenty-four hours per day, ready to respond to your needs immediately, and all of this subjects us to the ever-increasing costs of recruiting, educating, and retaining such personnel just as in any other field, (maybe even more so because of the nature of our profession.) The responsibility for sharing the ever-increasing cost of our local, state and federal governments through payment of taxes; the ever-increasing cost of merchandise, supplies and equipment affects us in the same degree that any other segment of our society experiences in its particular lines of endeavor. The costs of maintaining adequate facilities of a specialized, single-purpose nature which satisfy very exacting requirements of our state and local statutes must also be considered. These are all part of our basic overhead expenses involved for which we must be remunerated, beyond which people need advance only if they choose to do so of their own free will and accord.

There are at least two very definite parts which contribute to the cost of the funeral. The merchandise, services and facilities provided by the funeral director, and the 'banking' function performed by the funeral director, commonly referred to as 'cash advances,' where we help people buy cemetery lots, open graves, and do various and assorted other things that have absolutely no bearing upon our income or profit, but which we extend to the family as helping services at a time when its cash position may be strained, and/or, in a transitional state. It is not unusual for the deceased individual to be the only one who can sign checks, withdraw from a savings account, or whatever. So this is the other part. But unfortunately, when people refer to the funeral expense, those dramatic figures you sometimes hear quoted in relation to us might well be that total charge including cash advances, when actually as far as the funeral firm and the funeral director were concerned, it was really a modest, and in many cases, a minimal expense.

The Role of the Funeral Director

Objective analysis of the fact would reveal to you that funeral service, as a whole, has done a most commendable job of minimizing price advances during these past few decades compared to other fields, and one receives maximum service and merchandise value for dollars spent, from each and every one of us with which I am familiar.

The funeral is perhaps the most negative expense of a life time. Enjoyable expenses are paid over weekly, monthly, yearly periods. Not at all 'enjoyable,' the funeral bill comes in one lump sum with the buying public retaining no tangible 'merchandise,' so to speak after the burial. We even can call it a distasteful experience.

Now some people ask about anticipatory planning for the funeral. When death is imminent, is the funeral director prepared to help a person? In my mind, pre-planning is not where the funeral directors aggressively seek and advertise pre-arrangements. I prefer that the emphasis of funeral directors be upon informing families, throughout this country, of the many ways funeral service will accommodate their needs, at reasonable expense, when they come to the point of need; that it's not 'unusual' to 'feel' need, to seek advice in advance of death, to make an objective choice of a funeral director, call him, and confer with him. I would say that the funeral service practitioners of this country are quite prepared to be most helpful in relieving those we counsel of the many anxieties which occur when planning in advance. This could involve choosing a casket, or discussing the kind of service which might be available. At that point, the funeral director is most able to guide them through the entire experience. He will judge in many cases whether they're ready to choose a casket or, exactly how much they are ready to cope with at that point. (People come, but are not always ready.) If they come,

195

we know they're at least ready to become informed; maybe ready to plan the type of funeral they want to have, either for themselves or the individual for whom they're planning it; perhaps able to give us all the personal information that sometimes only they know. They may, also, be simply curious. They want to be reassured that funeral directors can accommodate every budget circumstances in which they might find themselves.

There are certain things that you have to understand about the funeral director when you ask him for help. Dr. Silverman referred to us as gatekeepers. We are just learning about this role, about referring people to additional services that they may need. If a funeral director agrees to give financial help to a program or to collaborate in developing a new program for the widowed, his efforts are likely to be misconstrued and regarded as a business venture. He is susceptible to criticism and will be seen as acting out of selfish motives. This may be why, when you approach many funeral directors, you may find them hesitant and uncooperative about getting involved. Rather than ask for help from your local funeral director, ask him to put you in touch with the Executive Secretary or Vice-President of the State Association. Here the message will be received correctly; there will be no problem about commercial or competitive motives since the organization represents the entire profession. The Association has to be certain that the effort undertaken is substantial; that it is worthwhile to cooperate. By talking to the individual funeral director and to the Association, you are making them aware of the problems of the bereaved, and the purpose of a Widow-to-Widow program. It is important for the widowed to recognize their own educational function as they seek collaborators.

196

In addition to the funeral director, I can think of several other contacts in the community that may give money as well as moral support to developing programs:

1—It may be useful to approach the Trust Departments of local commercial banks. This is the department which handles the widows' affairs. They know the widowed in their community. They have philanthropic programs as well, and often give small grants to service programs in their locales.

2—The local Chamber of Commerce may give some support. Don't expect them to do any work themselves . . . but they may offer some financial backing. They are under-staffed and you have to keep after them.

3—Your clergy should help you. You are really doing the work they should be doing, but they can only come as counsellors, you come with living experience. You really can say what the Lord meant to you. You can tell the clergy what it is like to be widowed, and what your needs are.

The challenge is to get out into the community where you live and work and make the needs of the widowed known. You have the power in your hand. There is a need—fill it—don't wait!

In conclusion, the funeral director is a very dedicated and often much misrepresented person. Yet when a death occurs, people have a change of attitude and are more willing to see him in a positive, helpful light. Widowed people know this. If you do work closely with the funeral director, if you call on him and get back to him in the areas where he can help you, you should find in him a friend who could be a tremendous boost to you in your service.

DISCUSSION NOTES

In the subsequent discussion, the idea of pre-planning was extended to explore the possibility of pre-paid funerals. The opportunity to obtain burial insurance varies from state to state. A man with an insurance background noted that some funeral directors in the past maneuvered people with burial insurance to sign uncontestable signatures of beneficiaries to the funeral director. These abuses, albeit by a very few, caused insurance commissions to draw tighter laws. However, he said, plans are again becoming available and in some places, men and women over 60 can buy insurance for $7.00 a month. He did point out that most reputable insurance salesmen will make arrangements to incorporate funds for burial and cemetery expenses in the policy or they will suggest that the individual put the cash in a position where it is available. One problem is to locate the bankbook when the need becomes real. People should have a record of where everything is. Someone else recalled the "Landsmanshaft" organizations of new immigrants which functioned as fraternal organizations. Membership entitled the individual to a cemetery plot and the funeral was pre-paid.

Attention then turned to a group which sells cemetery lots on a pre-need basis. The director of the group talked of his salesmen's experience:

> They go out in the community and sell pre-need cemetery lots to young families before they need them. The only way you can do that is if you can educate a family to understand the realities of the one experience that every family must go through at one time or another. It's a highly skilled thing to be able to take a 35-year-old man and his wife (who are perfectly

healthy, and would rather have wall-to-wall carpeting), sit them down, and make them come to grips for that evening with the proposition that it's a much better thing to prepare for death. We find, very often, that people who come to the cemetery and bury somebody in a pre-need lot, seem much more 'at ease or at peace with what has been done,' than, for example, the woman who has come to make an at-need purchase associated with grief, tragedy and separation. She's just finished choking the world symbolically on the funeral director's neck. She's out at the cemetery, sure that she's going to be taken there.

The discussion then focused on the subject of people's ability to express grief and on how others react when they do. A question was raised about the use of tranquilizers at the funeral so that people would remain composed. Several participants suggested it might be better if people released their feelings at this time instead of keeping them bottled up. If the bereaved are numb in the initial stage of grief, it may not be functional to depress them more. A man with many years of experience as a Navy Chaplain noted American men are trained, from the time they are very little, not to cry. Time and again, as the bearer of sad news to the families of servicemen, he encouraged them to cry, to unloose their feelings. This is especially true today when so many people have given up their traditions and do not have the security of knowing what to do anymore.

Various approaches to the funeral were discussed. Mr. Waring made the point that it is important to discover what the word "funeral" means to the bereaved. No two funerals are exactly alike. Different cultures have different funeral traditions. One member of the group commented on his unique position. He is Jewish but comes from a family of many practicing Episcopalians. He has had occasion to hear each group comment on the other's burial practices. His Episcopalian uncle thought the Jews barbaric to bury their dead within 24 hours of death with no chance to say, "Good-bye." After returning home from a wake, a Jewish relative thought the Episcopalians equally barbaric to have an open casket. The important issue is to help people come to grips with the reality of what has happened within the framework that is most acceptable to them. In this connection the value of the open coffin was discussed.

Mr. Waring felt that funeral directors always try:

> ... to keep an open mind about closed caskets. When someone asks for this, they're often saying they are fearful. In almost all cases, we recommend that relatives allow the friends, the living group in their community, to share this recognition experience with them. It may be done privately, or publicly, but it is healthiest for it to be done! If I can possibly help it, I will not allow a family to let a life depart from them without at least some member of a family, and particularly the one or two who are closest to it, to have a private moment (even if it's just five minutes in recognition of that person's death), with the person in the casket.

Some of the participants suggested that memorial services in which there is no coffin, to some extent, postponed the confrontation with the reality of the death. In the Jewish tradition, relatives are required to actually bury the deceased. It is their final act of respect and it is their obligation. At the same time, Jewish law prohibits the opening of the casket as a violation of the privacy of the deceased.

There was a difference of opinion about closing the casket in front of the family and lowering the coffin in their presence at the cemetery. Not everyone felt this confrontation was helpful. Even the funeral directors disagreed amongst themselves about what was the best procedure.

A mobile society encourages people to postpone making plans for their ultimate death. This discussion was summarized by the statement:

Facing death, whether you're a mobile person, or whether you're living in one community all your life, is something that's very real. It's not something one does easily ... one has to start to develop attitudes and a point of view that allows one to cope with this from the very outset of life. When we work with people who are bereaved and have faced this loss, they are a constant reminder to us that a death has occurred and we can't run away from this fact any longer. Thus they are stigmatized, if you will. We begin to get a picture that the funeral director has a real service to offer. He stands as an important gatekeeper ... his role is an evolving one at this point. I hope we develop an appreciation for his various roles and problems and return home to develop new collaborations, new coalitions to involve people in some of the broader perspectives required to serve the bereaved.

EPILOGUE

By Phyllis Silverman

The formal meetings covered only a small part of the learning which took place in these workshops. Most important in this week-end for the widowed was that they all had similar experiences which made everyone feel closer than would be expected in a group this size. Many people stayed up late into the night, talking about their feelings and problems and sharing ways in which they might be resolved.

We had talked a good deal in the meetings about serving the newly bereaved. However, there were personal problems which concerned most of the people present. These were related to making a new life for themselves. They had come to terms with the fact that they were, indeed, widowed—that the relationship with their spouse, possible only in the context of a marriage, was an historic fact, not relevant to their current life and to the satisfaction of their present needs. They wanted to discuss these personal dilemmas in an open forum, which I chaired. The notes from this short forum serve as an excellent epilogue to this book.

The key question was: What are the opportunities for finding satisfactions that were once available through marriage; how does a widowed person find substitutes or alternatives for these in other kinds of relationships? The discussion focused on the re-orientation of goals and life values, which become necessary as the widowed person realizes he or she is, indeed, alone.

One of the younger women, who voluntarily began the discussion, stated the problem very succinctly. She had been widowed four years, and her concerns were to find the things which help a widow continue to grow. She has found the thinking of the Women's Liberation Movement helpful to her in her adjustment to the single role. Their outlook was helpful in getting rid of the negative feelings attached to being a widow; the most prominent of which was that she was no longer complete. Women's Lib advocates that you are a whole person as a woman, and this is something most widows have to learn. Another widow said that, ideally, a person should have become independent before marriage. If a woman has a sense of herself and what she can do, it is easier to cope with being a widow.

In response to this, several women suggested that, in helping others, you are a whole person. You need to get involved, and in this involvement you find yourself as a person.

As the discussion proceeded, it became clear that it was not simply a question of being a "whole" person (whatever that means). People are afraid of the word "widow" as if it denotes something not whole. This is a feeling the widow has to get over. She has to learn to see herself as able to do things alone, and to successfully manage her own life. She has to learn to evaluate her goals and then seek direction for the way she wants to live her life to realize these goals. When she was married, her husband did this with her, or their goals were tied to his job and what it meant economically and socially for the family. What is now missing is a relationship that allows for sharing life. An individual is always whole—but what is lacking is the opportunity to satisfy the need to share.

As chairman, I summarized what I heard by sorting out the different needs people have. There seemed to be a need for involvement for example, which can be satisfied best by helping others. In a marriage, a wife takes care of her husband because she is involved with him. This need also can be met by taking care of children. However, there is another need, the need for human intimacy, and intimate sharing—not necessarily sexual, but an emotional and social intimacy as well—which seems possible only in a marital relationship. It is not clear how, or if, one finds satisfaction for this need in any other kind of relationship.

In response to this, one widow said:

> I always had the feeling that my 'way of life' now was temporary. Statistically, the facts being what they are, it may have to be permanent. This is something I don't know how to cope with.

In a very realistic tone, this was answered by:

> There is *no* substitute for the intimate sharing of marriage. It takes 'an act of will' for us to accept this reality. You can do many things, but the fulfillment is only for *you* now and there won't be anyone waiting at home to talk about it—as there once was.

The widowers present were less concerned with the permanence of their current status. Most of them felt they could remarry if they wanted to, and thought that they probably would. This alternative was, clearly, more available to them. The Catholic men referred briefly to the conflict their religion places them in when they consider satisfying their sexual needs outside of a marital relationship.

I saw the issue of independence as different from the issue of intimacy. The need to share has little to do with whether or not a woman is independent and self-directed or dependent in marriage. Even as we help a woman become less dependent, this does not do away with the other needs. There are alternative relationships with friends, and involvement with service to others which can provide an individual with a new sense of competence and wholeness. The question seems to be: To what extent can one have the sharing that takes place in marriage, which also brings with it emotional support and an order to one's daily life? No one knew how to find this, but it was clear that this is what the loneliness is about that everyone in the room reported feeling.

One response to all this was a reminder that each of the participants had been married once, that all of them were, therefore, better off than those who were never married. This widow felt that they had something special to offer as a widow. She said, "Take advantage of this new identity and go out and do what you can with it."

Bibliography

Abrahams, Ruby, "Mutual Help for the Widowed," *Social Work,* Vol. 17, Sept., 1972, pp. 54-61.

Agee, J., *A Death in the Family,* New York: Avon Publications, 1963.

Anthony, Sylvia, *The Child's Discovery of Death,* New York: Harcourt, Brace, 1940.

Arnstein, Helene S., *What to Tell Your Child About Birth, Illness, Death, Divorce and Other Family Crises,* Indianapolis: Bobbs-Merrill, 1962.

Beachy, W. N., "Assisting the Family in Time of Grief," *Journal of the American Medical Association,* 202 (November 6, 1967), pp. 559-560.

Beck, Frances, *Diary of a Widow,* Boston: Beacon Press, 1965.

Benda, Clemens, "Bereavement and Grief Work," *Journal of Pastoral Care,* 16 (Spring, 1962), pp. 1-13.

Best, Pauline, "An Experience on Interpreting Death to Children," *Journal of Pastoral Care* (1948), pp. 1, 2.

Bowlby, John, "Grief and Mourning in Infancy and Early Childhood," *The Psychoanalytic Study of the Child,* Vol. XV, New York: International University Press, 1960, pp. 9-52.

—————, "Process of Mourning," *International Journal of Psychoanalysis,* XLLL (1961), 329.

Bowers, Margaretta, *Conflicts of the Clergy,* New York: Thomas Nelson & Sons, 1973.

Budmen, Karl, "Grief and the Young: A Need to Know," *Archives of the Foundation of Thanatology,* I, 1 (1969), pp. 11-12.

Chaloner, L., "How to Answer the Questions Children Ask About Death," *Parents' Magazine,* XXXVII (November, 1962), pp. 48-49, 100, 102.

Champagne, Marion, *Facing Life Alone,* Indianapolis: Bobbs-Merrill, 1964.

Clayton, Paula, Lynn Desmarail, and George Winokur, "A Study of Normal Bereavement," *American Journal of Psychiatry,* Vol. 125, 2 (August, 1968).

Decker, Bea and Gladys Koorman, *After the Flowers Have Gone,* Michigan: Zondervan Corp., 1973.

Egleson, Jim and Janet T., *Parents Without Partners,* 1961, New York: Ace Star Books, 1961. (Paperback)

Feifel, Herman, (ed.), *The Meaning of Death,* New York: McGraw Hill Book Company, 1965.

Fulton, R. (ed.), *Death and Identity,* New York: John Wiley and Sons, 1965.

Gorer, Geoffrey, *Death, Grief and Mourning,* New York: Doubleday, 1967.

Goudge, Elizabeth, *A Book of Comfort,* Brooklyn, New York: Fontana, 1968.

Grollman, Earl A., *Explaining Death to Children,* Boston: Beacon Press, 1967.

—————, *Talking About Death: A Dialogue Between Parent and Child,* Boston: Beacon Press, 1970.

—————, *Suicide,* Boston: Beacon Press, 1971.

Habenstein, R. and Lamers, W., *The History of American Funeral Directing,* Milwaukee: Bulfin Printers, 1955.

Hunt, Morton M., *The World of the Formerly Married,* New York: McGraw Hill Book Company, 1966.

Ilgenfritz, Marjorie S., "Mothers on Their Own—Widows and Divorcees," *Marriage and Family Living,* XXIII (February, 1961), pp. 38-41.

Bibliography

Jackson, Edgar N., *Understanding Grief: Its Roots, Dynamics and Treatment,* New York: Abingdon-Cokesbury Press, 1957.

——————, *For The Living,* New York: Channel Press, 1963.

——————, *You and Your Grief,* New York: Channel Press, 1966.

Johnson, Mildred, *The Smiles and the Tears,* Old Tappan, New York: Fleming H. Revell Company, 1969.

Jones, Eva, *Raising Your Child in a Fatherless Home,* Glencoe, Ill.: The Free Press, 1963.

Kooiman, G., *When Death Takes a Father,* Grand Rapids, Michigan: Baker Book House, 1968.

Kreis, Bernardine and Pattie, Alice, *Up From Grief. Patterns Of Recovery,* New York: The Seabury Press, 1969.

Kutscher, Austin H., *But Not To Lose. A Book of Comfort for Those Bereaved,* New York: Frederick Fell, Inc., 1969.

——————, *Death And Bereavement,* Springfield, Illinois: Charles C. Thomas, 1969.

Langer, Marion, *Learning to Live as a Widow,* New York: Julian Messner, 1957.

Maddison, D. and Agnes Viola, "The Health of Widows in the Year Following Bereavement," *Journal of Psychosomatic Research,* Vol. 12 (July, 1968), pp. 292-306.

Marris, Peter, *Widows and Their Families,* London: Routledge and Kegan Paul, 1958.

Mathison, Jean, "A Cross-Cultural View of Widowhood," *Omega,* Vol. 1, No. 3 (August, 1970), pp. 201-218.

Moriarity, David M., (ed.), *The Loss of Loved Ones. The Effects of a Death in the Family on Personality Development,* Springfield, Illinois: Charles C. Thomas, 1967.

Morse, Theresa, *Life Is For Living,* New York: Double-day, 1973.

Murray, Dan, "Now I Walk Alone," as told by Mary East, *McCalls Magazine* (Fall, 1961), pp. 144-147.

Parkes, Colin Murray, *Bereavement,* London: International Universities Press, 1972.

Pastoral Psychology, Issue devoted to "The Widow, The Divorcée, and the Single Woman," XVIII (December, 1967).

Rosen, Roslyn, "The Other Side of Loneliness," *The Single Parent,* VIII (December, 1965), pp. 4-5 and 34.

Schlesinger, Benjamin, "The One Parent Family. Recent Literature," *Journal of Marriage and the Family,* XXVIII (February, 1966), pp. 103-109.

——————, *The One Parent Family. Perspectives and Annotated Bibliography,* Canada: University of Toronto Press, 1969.

Silverman, Phyllis, "Factors Involved in Accepting An Offer of Help," *Archives of the Foundation of Thanatology,* Vol. III, No. 3, Fall, 1971, pp. 161-171.

——————, "The Widow as a Caregiver in a Program of Preventive Intervention With Other Widows," *Mental Hygiene* (1970).

——————, "The Widow-to-Widow Program," *Mental Hygiene,* Vol. 53, No. 3 (July, 1969), p. 333.

——————, "Widowhood and Preventive Intervention," *Family Coordinator,* January, 1972, pp. 95-102.

Spiro, Jack Daniel, *A Time to Mourn: Judaism and the Psychology of Bereavement,* New York: Bloch Publishing Co., 1967.

Start, Clarissa, *When You're a Widow,* Saint Louis, London: Concordia Publishing House, 1968.

Streib, Gordon F., "The Social Involvement of American Widows," *American Behavioral Scientist,* Vol. XIV, No. 1 (September-October, 1970), pp. 25-41.

——————— and Thompson, W. E., "The Older Person in a Family Context," In C. Tibbitts (ed.), *Handbook of Social Gerontology,* Chicago: University of Chicago Press, 1960, pp. 447-488.

Strugnell, Cécile, *Adjustment to Widowhood and Some Related Problems, A Selective and Annotated Bibliography,* New York: Health Sciences Publishing Corp., 1974.
An extensive bibliography prepared to form a background for the Widow-to-Widow Research program, directed by Dr. Phyllis Silverman.

Taves, Isabella, *Women Alone,* New York: Funk and Wagnalls, 1968.

Torre, Marie, "How I Survived," As told by Edie Adams, *Redbook,* 46 (September, 1962), pp. 94-97.

Torrie, Margaret, *Begin Again. A Book for Women Alone,* London: J. M. Dent and Sons, Ltd., 1970. (Author is founder of Cruse Club in London.) (See also Cruse publications.)

——————— , "Meeting Widows' Problems," *Toc. H. Journal* (May, 1963).

Townsend, P., *The Family Life of Old People,* London: Routledge and Kegan Paul, 1967, pp. 41-44, 132-133, 174-176.

Tunstall, J., *Old And Alone,* London: Routledge and Kegan Paul, 1966, pp. 45-50, 91-93, 142-155.

Tyhurst, J. S., "The Rule of Transition States—Including Disasters—in Mental Illness," in *Symposium on Preventive and Social Psychiatry* (Washington, D.C.: U.S. Government Printing Office, 1958), pp. 149-169.

211

Wallant, Edward L., *The Human Season*, New York: Harcourt, Brace, 1960.

Wolf, Anna W. M., *Helping Your Child Understand Death*, New York: Child Study Association, 1958.

Wolff, S., *Children Under Stress*, Allen Lande, 1969.